Illustrator:
Phil Hopkin

Editor:
Mary Kaye Taggart

Editorial Project Manager:
Karen J. Goldfluss, M.S. Ed.

Editor in Chief:
Sharon Coan, M.S. Ed.

Art Director:
Elayne Roberts

Associate Designer:
Denise Bauer

Cover Artist:
Chris Macabitas

Product Manager:
Phil Garcia

Imaging:
Ralph Olmedo, Jr.

Publishers:
Rachelle Cracchiolo, M.S. Ed.
Mary Dupuy Smith, M.S. Ed.

Conflict RESOLUTION

GRADES K-4

Author:

Julia Jasmine, M.A.

Teacher
Created
Materials

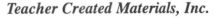

Teacher Created Materials, Inc.
P.O. Box 1040
Huntington Beach, CA 92647
ISBN-1-59690-103-3

©1997 Teacher Created Materials, Inc.   Made in U.S.A.

Table of Contents

Introduction

Conflict Resolution is more than just a book of techniques for resolving conflicts. It is, first and foremost, a systematic program designed to show teachers methods that will help their students to ward off or even bypass many conflicts altogether. It also presents nonviolent ways (assertiveness, negotiation, compromise, and mediation) to resolve the conflicts that do occur.

This program will take teachers and their students (grade levels K-4) through five steps: developing good self-concepts, growing in social awareness, acquiring communication skills, using techniques for conflict resolution, and finally, developing respect and empathy for others. In addition, age-appropriate concerns will also be addressed. Students in kindergarten and grades one and two will participate in activities that will help them move from parallel play to the beginning of cooperative groups. Older students in grades three and four will also begin to consider the relationships among these important concepts: competition and cooperation, rules and self-direction, equal treatment and special circumstances, and justice and compassion. A bonus thematic unit on friendship is also included.

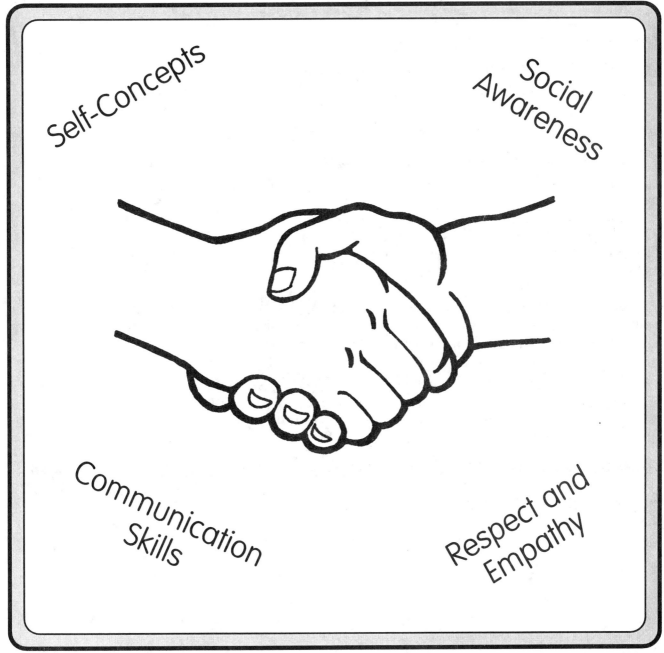

How to Use This Book

Conflict Resolution is organized by grade level—kindergarten, first grade/second grade, and third grade/fourth grade. The topics and subtopics repeat at each level. The activities for each topic and subtopic are different and developmentally appropriate for each level. Depending on the group of students you are teaching, their age, maturity, and experience, you can choose activities from any of the levels to suit your needs and still cover the main topics.

The first topic at each level is *Who Am I?* **Developing Self-Concepts**. Most experts in child development agree that the development of self-concepts, including self-esteem, is a basic step in getting along with others. If children, or adults for that matter, do not see themselves as separate and valuable, they cannot see others as separate and valuable either. In these sections, students are given the opportunity to get to know themselves better.

The second topic at each level, *Who Are You?* **Growing in Social Awareness**, directs the students to focus on others. This is a huge step for kindergartners. Older students who may already be very social often need help in directing their social skills in a constructive way. In these sections, students are given the opportunity to get to know each other.

The third topic, *Can We Talk?* **Acquiring Communication Skills**, deals with an area that is often taken for granted. Just because people are able to talk does not mean that they can communicate! Students can be taught the basics of communication, thus increasing their abilities to understand one another.

The fourth topic, *Can We Get Along?* **Using Techniques for Conflict Resolution**, gives students some real tools to use in dealing with disagreements, from the smallest argument to the most potentially dangerous dispute.

The fifth topic, *Why Should We Care?* **Developing Respect and Empathy**, helps students to take a look at the fact that everyone has the right to his or her own opinions and that everyone feels the same emotions.

The sections entitled *Are We Making Progress?* **Age Appropriate Concerns** deal with the development of cooperative learning from kindergarten through second grade. At grades three and four this section is based on the fact that children in this age group are beginning to feel strongly about the importance of competition, the necessity for rules, the value of equal treatment, and the significance of justice. Although there is certainly nothing wrong with these standards for behavior, it is important that students also recognize the relevance of cooperation, self-direction, special circumstances, and compassion. This section gives students an opportunity to compare these qualities and determine when one is more appropriate than another in a given situation.

At the end of the book you will find a **Bonus Section** consisting of **A Thematic Unit on Friendship**. It could be equally effective used as an orientation for the activities in this book or, at the end, as a culmination and celebration of what your students have learned.

Kindergarten

Developing Self-Concepts

My Name: I Can Find My Name

Purpose:

to help students think of their names as their personal property, to learn to recognize their names in written form, and to use them to identify things that are theirs (such as their "cubbies")

Materials:

- ◆ at least three strips for each student (page 7)
- ◆ special badges, one for each child (page 7)
- ◆ a marker
- ◆ scissors
- ◆ safety pins

Activity—Part 1:

Before starting this activity, use a marker to print each child's name on at least three name strips. Cut out the name strips. Place two of the name strips for each student around the room in different places. (If each child has a cubby, lay an appropriate name strip near the front of each one.)

Begin this activity during your circle time. Talk with your whole class about names, their own names and names in general. Then give each child his or her own name strip to look at. Have them notice the letters and how they look.

Ask who would like to start. Have a volunteer take his or her name strip and go around the room looking for the strips that match it. The student can then bring the matching strips back to the circle to display.

After one student has demonstrated the activity, let the rest of the students hunt for their names. When everyone has found his or her name strips and displayed them in the circle, collect the strips in preparation for extending the activity the next day.

Repeat Part 1 of this activity until all can easily match their names and feel comfortable with the task.

Activity—Part 2:

Place the name strips around the room again. Increase the challenge of the activity by asking your students to again hunt for their own names but without a sample matching strip in their hands. Reward their successes with praise and with the presentation of special badges.

Evaluation and Processing:

Let your students discuss how they feel about being able to recognize their names. Is it a good feeling? Where would they like to see their names written? What can they do with this accomplishment? (find their cubbies, locate their drawings and other papers, etc.)

Developing Self-Concepts

My Name: I Can Find My Name

Teacher Directions: Print each child's name on at least three strips and then cut the strips out. Recognize the students' successes by handing out the badges below. Carefully attach them with safety pins.

I can find my name!

I can find my name!

Developing Self-Concepts

How I Look: Drawing My Self-Portrait

Purpose:

to help students think about how they look and how their faces are special and different from each other's faces

Materials:

- several mirrors
- large white drawing paper
- crayons (try to get a variety of skin and hair colors)
- extra name strips from the previous lesson
- pins or tape

Activity—Part 1:

Your circle time is a good time to begin this activity. Pass mirrors around the circle and have each child take a good look at himself or herself. How do they know they are seeing their own faces? What makes each person different and special? Have them look at their hair, their eyes, their noses, and their mouths. Let them discuss their observations.

Next, have the children sit at tables where they will have large sheets of paper and a selection of crayons. Tell your students to choose colors that show how they really look and to make their drawings life size. (Some students will draw teeny, tiny pictures on the large sheets of paper. This may be a reflection of their drawing style or it may demonstrate how they feel about their own importance in the world. Although certainly not a conclusive psychological indicator, it can alert you to the necessity for helping a child build his or her self-esteem.)

Activity—Part 2:

While the students are drawing, post their name strips on the bulletin board or in different places around the room where you plan to display their self-portraits. As the students finish, have them take their drawings and find their own names. They can stand by their names while you go around to pin or tape up their pictures.

Evaluation and Processing:

Take time to enjoy and appreciate your new art gallery. Ask your students . . . What did you like best about this activity? Was it hard or easy? Does your picture look like you? If you did it again, would you use the same colors? Was it fun to be able to find your name on the wall or bulletin board?

Developing Self-Concepts

What I Know: What I Know How to Do

Purpose:

to help students think about the things they already know how to do and the things that they can look forward to mastering based on grade-level expectations

Materials:

◆ kindergarten checklist (use the checklist on page 10 or make up one based on your own school or district lists)

◆ red and blue crayons

Activity—Part 1:

During your circle time show your students the checklist and its boxes. Discuss the things they already know how to do and the things that they can look forward to learning. Show them how to fill in a box with a crayon. Have them use red to indicate the things they already know and blue for the things they are going to learn.

Next, have the children sit at tables and pass out checklists and crayons. Point out the boxes under the heading "Now." (It would be nice to have an aide or classroom helper to walk around during this activity to help the students stay in the correct column.) Read each item from the checklist out loud and give your students enough time to decide if this is something they already know how to do. If they do know how to do this item tell them, "Use your red crayon to fill in the box." If they do not know how to do the item, have them use their blue crayons. Complete the rest of the checklist column in the same manner.

Collect the completed checklists and put them away for use in Part 2 of this activity.

Activity—Part 2:

You will know when to expect all of the students in your class to have mastered the items on the checklist. If anyone is having trouble with a particular skill, you can devote some time to that skill and that student before using the checklist for the second time. The idea, of course, is to have all of your students color all of the new boxes red.

At the appropriate time toward the end of the school year, show the students the checklists and remind them of how they colored in the boxes. Then repeat the activity, except have the students fill in the column headed "Later." Walk around the room while this is being done to make sure that everyone is coloring the boxes red. If someone is considering using a blue crayon, stop and ask why. If necessary, have the student who is hesitating demonstrate the skill in question for his or her own satisfaction.

Send the checklists home with the students or post them around the classroom for everyone to see.

Evaluation and Processing:

Encourage the children to enjoy their successes. Ask the students . . . Which skills were the easiest and which were the hardest? Which skills were the most enjoyable? Which skills made them feel the proudest of themselves?

Developing Self-Concepts

What I Know: What I Know How to Do

Name _____

Directions: Use a red crayon to fill in the boxes by the items that you do know how to do. Use a blue crayon to fill in the boxes by the items that you do not know how to do.

Skill	Now	Later
1. I can jump.	☐	☐
2. I can hop.	☐	☐
3. I can skip.	☐	☐
4. I can button.	☐	☐
5. I can zip.	☐	☐
6. I can tie a bow.	☐	☐
7. I can look at books.	☐	☐
8. I can talk about pictures.	☐	☐
9. I can listen to stories.	☐	☐
10. I can find my name.	☐	☐
11. I can count to ten.	☐	☐
12. I can name a circle and a square.	☐	☐

Developing Self-Concepts

How I Feel: My Feelings

Purpose:

to help students identify and express their feelings

Materials:

- ◆ copies of page 12 (or make your own), one for each student
- ◆ copies of page 13, one copy for each student
- ◆ scissors
- ◆ glue sticks

Activity—Part 1:

Before beginning this activity cut out one set of page 13 for each student. This would be the perfect time to employ the help of a volunteer parent!

During circle time encourage your students to talk about their feelings. Show them the faces that represent various feelings (page 13). Talk about the feelings. Ask such questions as these: How do you feel when you are happy? What about when you are sad or angry? Is there a difference between feeling surprised and feeling scared? What is it?

Next, have the children sit at tables and pass out the response sheets (page 12), piles of faces, and glue sticks. Point out the squares which indicate where the faces should be glued. (It would be nice to have an aide or classroom helper to walk around during this activity to help the students.) Read each item from the response sheet aloud and give your students enough time to decide on the faces that match the way they feel. Assure them that any choice is "correct."

Collect the completed checklists and put them away for use in Part 2 of this activity.

Activity—Part 2:

Repeat the entire activity at intervals during the year. Compare answers to see which feelings have changed and which have stayed the same.

Evaluation and Processing:

Encourage, but do not require, students to discuss their feelings. Investigate responses that concern you in a tactful way. For example, if a student feels sad or mad about coming to school, you may be able to find out why and correct the situation without making that student feel he or she has done something wrong or inappropriate.

Developing Self-Concepts

How I Feel: My Feelings

Name_____

Directions: Glue a face below each sentence to show how you feel.

1. When I come to school, I feel	2. When I go home, I feel
3. When I learn something, I feel	4. When something good happens, I feel
5. When it's time to share, I feel	6. When I get a present, I feel

Developing Self-Concepts

How I Feel: My Feelings

Happy	Happy	Happy
Happy	Sad	Sad
Mad	Mad	Surprised
Surprised	Scared	Scared

Developing Self-Concepts

My Family: This Is My Family

Purpose:

to validate students' memberships in families and to acknowledge differences in family structures

Materials:

- ◆ a large supply of old magazines
- ◆ scissors
- ◆ construction paper
- ◆ glue sticks

Activity—Part 1:

Before starting this activity, send home a letter requesting donations of used magazines. Make sure that the parents know that they will not be getting the magazines back.

Begin this activity during your circle time by discussing family relationships. Talk about mothers, fathers, stepmothers, stepfathers, aunts, uncles, cousins, grandparents, etc. Find out if your students know that an aunt is the sister of a mother or father and an uncle is the brother of a mother or father. Ask other relationship questions such as these: What is a grandparent? What is a stepparent? What is a cousin? Do people have to live with you to be part of your family? Do all families have the same set of family members?

Leaf through a magazine or two to show your students how to look for people who remind them of their family members. Model the activity by finding pictures that remind you of your own family, cutting them out, and arranging them on a sheet of construction paper. (Do not forget to include yourself!)

Next, have the children sit at tables. Provide them with stacks of magazines, scissors, construction paper, and glue sticks. Encourage your students to find and cut out (with help, if necessary) pictures that look like, or could at least represent, their family members. They can then glue them onto their sheets of construction paper. Remind the children to include themselves in the family group. Post the finished family portraits on the bulletin board for the students to look at and talk about.

Activity—Part 2:

After a few days have passed, ask the students to talk about the pictures. Do all of the families have the same members? What different types of families are represented by the pictures? Write them on the board (mother-father-son-daughter, mother-daughter-grandmother, etc.) and then talk about why they are all families.

Note: If you have children who live in group homes or foster-family situations, you may want to skip Part 2 of this activity. Do whatever will be most comfortable for those students.

Evaluation and Processing:

Encourage, but do not require, your students to discuss the different types of families and why families are important.

 **Who Am I?**

Developing Self-Concepts

My Friends: My Friend Is . . .

Purpose:

to help students understand what friends are

Materials:

- ◆ large paper for painting on an easel
- ◆ easels
- ◆ brushes
- ◆ tempera paint
- ◆ fine black felt pens
- ◆ painting smocks or old shirts

Activity—Part 1:

Begin this activity during your circle time by discussing what the words "friends" and "friendship" mean. Ask such questions as . . . What are friends? Are there different kinds of friends? Can friends be different ages? Can people have more than one friend? Have you ever had an imaginary friend? What is an imaginary friend? Can a stuffed animal be a friend?

Have your students paint a picture of a friend. Let the paintings dry and save them for Part 2 of this activity.

Activity—Part 2:

Call on one child at a time to tell you about his or her picture. Using a fine black felt pen, write at the bottom of the picture what the child dictates to you. (Aides or classroom helpers could help during this aspect of the activity.) To help things run more efficiently, ask the children to be thinking of their stories while they wait for their turns.

Have each child share his or her picture with the rest of the class. Give the necessary help in reading the dictated story.

Let your students take their paintings home to share with their families.

Evaluation and Processing:

Encourage the students to give each other positive feedback on their pictures and stories. Ask . . . What did you like best about this activity? What were the easiest and hardest parts? If you were to do it again, would you do anything differently?

Growing in Social Awareness

Names: I Know Your Name

Purpose:

to help students become aware of others as individuals and to foster a sense of community in the classroom

Materials:

- ◆ first names of students printed on individual strips (use the strips on page 17 or make your own)
- ◆ double-sided tape to stick the strips onto the students
- ◆ small rewards (such as stickers)
- ◆ special badges, one for each child (page 17)
- ◆ safety pins

Activity—Part 1:

Begin this activity during circle time. Remind your students of how they learned to recognize their own names. Tell them that they will be playing games to help them learn the names of every student in the class. (You might also mention that there will be prizes!)

Attach the appropriate name strip to each student with double-sided tape. Have each student stand up in the circle, point to his or her name strip, and say, "I'm . . . ." When all of the students have introduced themselves and are sitting down, tell them that they will need to raise their hands to participate in this game. Walk around the outside of the circle. Stop behind one student and say, "Who knows this student's name?" Choose a student who raises his or her hand. If the correct name is given, hand both students a small reward and go on around the circle. Choose at least five sets of students. You can repeat this as a sponge activity any day at any time. The children do not have to be seated in a circle. Next, play "Name, Name, . . . !" like "Duck, Duck, Goose!" One child goes around the circle lightly tapping people on the head and saying, "Name, name, name . . . " until he or she says the actual name of the one touched. That person gets up, runs, and tries to tag the tapper. If the person who did the tapping is caught, he or she is "it" again just as in Duck, Duck, Goose! If he or she safely sits in the empty space, the person who was tapped continues the game.

Repeat these games at frequent intervals until your students seem to be calling each other by their names most of the time.

Activity—Part 2:

When you think the children are ready, ask for a volunteer to try to name everyone. Have this brave person start out next to you and go around the circle naming everyone. Reward everyone who tries. Give a special badge to everyone who succeeds. Play this game every morning or at every circle time until all of the students earn their badges. Then repeat it at intervals to keep the names firmly in mind.

Evaluation and Processing:

Let your students talk about how they feel about knowing all of the students' names. Is it a good, grown-up sort of feeling? Are they glad when others call them by name too?

Growing in Social Awareness

Names: I Know Your Name

Teacher Directions: Print each child's name on a name strip. Copy and cut out enough badges so that each student may have one. Use safety pins to attach the badges to clothing.

I Know All of the Names!

I Know All of the Names!

I Know All of the Names!

I Know All of the Names!

Growing in Social Awareness

Faces: Partner Portraits

Purpose:

to help students become aware of others as individuals and to support a positive attitude toward diversity in the classroom

Materials:

- large paper for painting on an easel
- easels
- brushes
- chairs for the students whose portraits are being painted
- tempera paints (try to provide many skin and hair colors along with the other usual colors)
- large empty picture frames, enough for half the students to use at one time (you can cut them out of cardboard)
- black markers
- painting smocks or old shirts

Activity—Part 1:

Before starting this activity spend some time mixing up paint in the skin tones and hair colors that your students will need to paint their portraits.

Divide your class into partners and have them sit next to each other in a circle. Tell the students to take a really good look at their partners, noticing exactly how they look—the color of their skin and eyes, the color of their hair and the way it grows, what they are wearing, etc. Ask several students to stand and hold empty picture frames up in front of them to show what should be included in a portrait and how big the pictures should be in relation to the students.

Help the children decide on the colors of paint they will use. Set up each pair with an easel and a chair and have them take turns painting each other's portraits. The person being painted should hold up a frame to help the partner focus on what should be included in the painting. Print each child's name at the bottom of the portraits (for example, Marissa by Tony).

Activity—Part 2:

Make an art gallery in the classroom where all of the portraits can be displayed. Take the time to admire and enjoy them. Model the types of comments you would like to hear: "Tony got the color of Marissa's hair exactly right." "Polly chose a color that matches Ben's skin." Have the students stand next to the portraits of themselves so that everyone can admire the results.

Evaluation and Processing:

Discuss the activity . . . Was it hard or easy to paint a portrait? Were you able to find the right colors? Did the person you painted like the painting? Did you like the painting your partner made of you? Would you like to do this kind of activity again?

Growing in Social Awareness

Qualities: The Right Word

Purpose:

to help students become aware of others as individuals and to support a positive awareness of personal qualities

Materials:

◆ copies of pages 20–23, several sets

◆ painted portraits from the previous lesson

Activity—Part 1:

Display a set of pages 20–23 during circle time and, as you name the words, let the students discuss each one and talk about what it means. If someone says, for example, "That's like Sarah," stop and say "It is like Sarah. Let's put this word on the bulletin board next to Sarah's portrait." (If no one compares a word to a classmate, you can do it yourself.)

Continue with the activity until everyone in the class has a word. (If you need others, use the blanks on page 23.)

Activity—Part 2:

Take time to enjoy the art gallery again, now with the addition of the new "right" words. Read each child's name aloud and comment on his or her word: Here is Maria. Maria is *helpful*.

Ask students if they would like to add another word somewhere. Would they like to give themselves another word? Do they think a classmate needs another word?

Evaluation and Processing:

Discuss the activity . . . How do you feel about your word? Does it feel like you? We can do this again in a few weeks and see if anyone needs another word.

Growing in Social Awareness

Qualities: The Right Word

Kind

| Generous |

| Exciting |

| Funny |

| Happy |

Growing in Social Awareness

Qualities: The Right Word

Cheerful

Nice

Truthful

Polite

Neat

Growing in Social Awareness

Qualities: The Right Word

Smart

Good

Helpful

Caring

Busy

Growing in Social Awareness

Qualities: The Right Word

Brave

Calm

Sweet

Growing in Social Awareness

Similarities: Everybody Eats

Purpose:

to help students become aware of and focus on the ways they are alike through the experience of foods (in this case, bread) from around the world

Materials:

- ◆ *Bread, Bread, Bread* by Anna Morris (Lothrop, Lee and Shepard, 1989)
- ◆ world map
- ◆ globe
- ◆ a few stems of wheat with the heads still attached and some dried corn (you can find these in craft shops)
- ◆ flour (in a bowl)
- ◆ corn meal (in a bowl)
- ◆ various types of breads (optional)
- ◆ bread dough (make or buy frozen and let it rise in the classroom)

Activity—Part 1:

Bread, Bread, Bread is a perfect choice for sharing during story time. It shows one of the ways that people all over the world are the same—they eat bread in some form.

Pass around the wheat and the corn. Let the students feel the flour and the cornmeal. Then read *Bread Bread, Bread* all the way through, displaying the wonderful photographs as you go. Then go back and study each picture. Refer to the helpful index for more information. Find all of the mentioned places on a map and/or globe.

As you look at the pictures in the book, ask your students which of the kinds of bread they have eaten. If possible, get an assortment of breads for the children to sample as they look at the pictures and find the places shown in the book.

Activity—Part 2:

Give your students the opportunity to see bread dough rise. If you are making the dough, mix it in the classroom. If you are using frozen dough, have it thawed and at the point where it will start to rise. (Placing the bowl of dough on an electric heating pad is a good way to make it rise.) Check the dough now and then during the rising time so that your students can see the process. If possible, bake the bread in the oven of your school's kitchen and share the resulting loaf with the students. Be sure to tell them that not all bread is made with yeast, but it is the yeast which makes this type of bread rise.

Evaluation and Processing:

Discuss the activity . . . Did you know there were so many kinds of bread? Which kind of bread is your favorite? Which types do you have at home? Does anyone at your house ever bake bread? What will you tell your family about what we did in school today? (Have your students practice what they will tell their families to reinforce the lesson. They can start out by saying "People from all over the world eat bread.")

Growing in Social Awareness

Differences: Everybody Eats

Purpose:

to help students become aware of and consider the ways they are different through the experience of foods (in this case, rice) as it is prepared in different cultures

Materials:

- ◆ *Everybody Cooks Rice* by Norah Dooley (Carolrhoda Books, 1991)
- ◆ world map
- ◆ globe
- ◆ uncooked and cooked rice
- ◆ copies of page 26, one for each student
- ◆ rice dishes (made by parents from the recipes given in *Everybody Cooks Rice*)
- ◆ copies of page 27, one for each student
- ◆ pictures of the countries represented by rice dishes (Barbados, Puerto Rico, Vietnam, India, China, Haiti, and Italy)

Activity—Part 1:

This activity can be as simple or as enriched as you want to make it. You can simply read the book and talk about the ways in which people are different based on their preparations of rice. You can show your students a quantity of uncooked rice and then show them what that same quantity of rice looks like after it has been cooked. Or, you can go all the way by having a Rice Festival.

Everybody Cooks Rice is a wonderful book about cultural diversity. It takes place in a multicultural community in the United States. Carrie goes looking for her little brother, and as she goes from house to house in her neighborhood, she is invited to sample the rice dishes being cooked for dinner. Read the book to your class. It has only 27 pages and can easily be read in one sitting. Talk about the different rice dishes. Have your students ever eaten any of them? Find the featured countries on a map and/or globe. If you are going to let your students observe the difference between uncooked and cooked rice, this would be a good time to do it.

Activity—Part 2:

Send home the letter on page 26 with copies of the recipes in the book. If you get a good response, plan to have a Rice Festival, a party with a buffet of the rice dishes, pictures of the countries represented, and maybe even dances, songs, and games. (A good source for these is *Musical Games for Children of All Ages* by Esther L. Nelson, Sterling Publishing, 1976.)

Evaluation and Processing:

Discuss Part 1 of the activity . . . Who can retell the story we read? Does Carrie have nice neighbors? What countries did they come from? Can you find these countries on the map? What happens to rice when it is cooked?

Discuss Part 2 of the activity . . . Did you enjoy our Rice Festival? Which rice dish did you like best?

Growing in Social Awareness

Differences: Everybody Eats

Dear Parents,

We are planning a Rice Festival based on a book that we have just read, *Everybody Cooks Rice*. The book features rice dishes from seven different countries: Barbados, Puerto Rico, Vietnam, India, China, Haiti, and Italy.

We are hoping to find some interested parents who will volunteer to make these rice dishes and bring them to school for our party. (Parents will also be invited.) Recipes for all of the dishes are attached to this letter. If you would like to make one of them for us, fill out the bottom of this letter and send it with your child to school.

We are planning to have our Rice Festival on_____at_____.

Sincerely,

_____

- -

Name_____

Student's Name _____

Phone Number_____

Rice Dish _____

Comments or Questions _____

_____

_____

_____

_____

Growing in Social Awareness

Differences: Everybody Eats

Growing in Social Awareness

Our Manners: Magic Words

Purpose:

to help students see manners as a way of recognizing the importance of other people and as a way to make others feel comfortable

Materials:

- ◆ *Grover's Guide to Good Manners* by Constance Allen (A Sesame Street/Golden Book, 1992)
- ◆ situation cards (pages 29 and 30)
- ◆ small rewards (stickers, stars, candies, etc.)

Activity—Part 1:

Read and discuss *Grover's Guide to Good Manners* during your story time. All of your students will probably already know the character of Grover from Sesame Street and should find it easy to relate to his advice. Grover sticks pretty close to the standard "magic words" children are asked to use: please, thank you, you're welcome, excuse me, and so on. As you read the book and display the pictures, ask for volunteers to act out the situations, assuming the roles of the characters in the book.

Activity—Part 2:

Talk with the children about using manners in school. Are manners just special words that we learn ahead of time? No, sometimes manners are words and actions that we use to make people feel good. Use the situation cards (pages 29 and 30) to demonstrate. Read a card out loud to the students in the circle. Ask for volunteers to act it out.

Depending on your students, you might want to try a variation on this lesson which you could call "Good Manners/Bad Manners." Have one set of volunteers act out the wrong things to say and do and another set act out the correct things or have the same set of volunteers act out both ways.

Use the blank cards on page 30 to write some situations that are appropriate for your classroom.

Be on the lookout for examples of good manners as they occur in your classroom and hand out rewards on the spot.

Evaluation and Processing:

Discuss the activity . . . Who can finish these sentences? "Having good manners is another way of being . . . ." (*kind, nice, thoughtful, polite,* etc.) "Using good manners makes our classroom a_____place to be." (*happy, safe, comfortable*)

Growing in Social Awareness

Our Manners: Magic Words

Teacher Directions: Read these cards to the children and either discuss the answers or have the children act out their answers. The blank cards at the bottom of page 30 are available for you to write your own situations.

Your friend was putting away the blocks and dropped them on the way to the block box. Some of them rolled under the table. What should you say?	A new boy came to school today and joined your class. He does not know where anything is, and he looks kind of scared. What should you say?
You fell off the swing at recess. You did not get hurt, but you knocked someone else down. What should you say?	Someone was making a really tall tower out of blocks in the classroom. When you walked by, you accidentally knocked it down. What should you say?
One of your classmates lost a paper that she was supposed to take home. She is crying. What should you say?	Your teacher has misplaced her glasses and is looking all over for them. What should you say?
Your friend's tooth just came out. He is not sure what to do. What should you say?	One of your classmates has a runny nose and no tissue. What should you say?

Growing in Social Awareness

Our Manners: Magic Words

Your friend forgot his money for a snack. You brought a snack from home and have enough for both of you. What should you say?	One of your classmates is upset because his dog ran away. He called for him and called for him, but he still had not come home when the school bus came. What should you say?
Today is your friend's birthday. His mother is sick so he cannot have a party. What should you say?	One of your classmates is worried about having to go to the dentist. You remember how you felt when you were going to the dentist. What should you say?
_____ _____ _____ _____ What should you say?	_____ _____ _____ _____ What should you say?
_____ _____ _____ _____ What should you say?	_____ _____ _____ _____ What should you say?

Acquiring Communication Skills

Sending: I Feel . . .

Purpose:

to give students information about and practice in sending clear messages when they communicate orally

Materials:

- several sets of masks (pages 32–36)
- rulers or paint stirrers
- tape
- assorted hand puppets

Activity—Part 1:

This activity is designed to help your students express themselves in "I" messages in order to communicate their feelings to others. They will do this through the use of masks and puppets.

Place a few sets of masks on the floor in the middle of the circle. Then introduce a non-threatening topic. For example, you might say, "It is raining today. How do you feel when it rains? Pick up a mask to show us and then tell us, using words. You can hold the mask in front of your face if you want to." (Model the type of responses you want in order to get things started: "I feel sad when it rains," "I feel happy when it rains," etc.) After a student has given an "I" message say, "Why do you feel sad (or happy, etc.) when it rains?" (Model this part too: "Because I can't play outside" or "Because rain makes the flowers grow," and so on.)

Use hand puppets to express "I" messages. The frog puppet might say, "I am a frog. I feel hoppy." The bee puppet might say, "I am a bee. I feel busy." Hand out puppets and have the students make up what they could say. Tell them to use this formula: "I am a_____. I feel_____."

Activity—Part 2:

When the children are comfortable with the masks and know the formula for an "I" message, encourage them to use sharing time in the circle to pick up a mask and express any feeling they want to. "Stand up or raise your hand if you want to tell us how you are feeling today." Be prepared for painful feelings as well as happy ones. Use this same technique to encourage your students to express their feelings about things that happen in the classroom. Model it yourself to help students understand how to do it: "I feel sad when I see Mary push Sally" or "I feel happy when Joey takes turns."

Evaluation and Processing:

Discuss the activity . . . What part did you like best—the masks or the puppets? Does it feel good to be able to tell us about how you feel? How do you feel right now?

Acquiring Communication Skills

Sending: I Feel . . .

Teacher Directions: Cut out the mask and mount it on heavy paper or cardboard. Cut out holes for the eyes. Tape a paint stirrer or ruler to the back.

Can We Talk?

Acquiring Communication Skills

Sending: I Feel . . .

Teacher Directions: Cut out the mask and mount it on heavy paper or cardboard. Cut out holes for the eyes. Tape a paint stirrer or ruler to the back.

Acquiring Communication Skills

Sending: I Feel . . .

Teacher Directions: Cut out the mask and mount it on heavy paper or cardboard. Cut out holes for the eyes. Tape a paint stirrer or ruler to the back.

Acquiring Communication Skills

Sending: I Feel . . .

Teacher Directions: Cut out the mask and mount it on heavy paper or cardboard. Cut out holes for the eyes. Tape a paint stirrer or ruler to the back.

Acquiring Communication Skills

Sending: I Feel . . .

Teacher Directions: Cut out the mask and mount it on heavy paper or cardboard. Cut out holes for the eyes. Tape a paint stirrer or ruler to the back.

 *Can We Talk?*

Acquiring Communication Skills

Receiving: I Hear . . .

Purpose:

to give students information about and practice in listening in order to receive clear oral messages

Materials:

◆ tapes of environmental sounds, natural and man-made (You can buy these or make your own.)

◆ teacher script (page 38)

◆ hand puppets

Activity—Part 1:

This activity is designed to help the children focus on their listening skills by providing opportunities to identify environmental sounds and by listening to "I" messages. At this point when the students listen to the "I" messages, they will only be listening for what is actually said rather than making judgments about the messages.

Play the tapes of environmental sounds for your students. Go through the tapes several times to help your students identify the sounds they hear. Depending on where you live, the children may not have previously heard all of the sounds. When they are familiar with all of the sounds, play a sound identification game.

Remind the students of the "I" messages that they have been practicing. Use hand puppets to review. Make the frog puppet say his lines. "I am a frog. I feel hoppy." Then ask the students to tell the frog what they heard him say: "You are saying that you feel hoppy." Continue with various puppets.

During the day state some "I" messages yourself: "I feel very excited about the way you picked up!" Then ask the students, "What can you hear? I can hear that you feel happy."

Activity—Part 2:

Use the script on another day. Read the "I" messages and the two response choices aloud. Ask the students which response a "good listener" would pick. Discuss both responses. Point out that the good listener lets the person have his or her own feelings. The other response tells the person how he or she should feel.

Evaluation and Processing:

Watch your students to see if they have internalized the active listening habit. You can see this when people share in your circle time. ("I feel happy because my uncle gave me a new doll." "You are saying that you feel happy," or "You are really lucky. I wish I had a new doll.")

Acquiring Communication Skills

Receiving: I Hear . . .

Teacher Directions: This page is a script for the teacher. Read the "I" messages and then read the two responses. Let the students choose which responses a good listener would say.

"I" Message	Active Listening	Judgment
I feel sad when I can't tie my shoes.	You are saying that you are sad.	You should just try harder!
I feel angry when someone pushes me.	I can hear that you are angry.	Just push him back!
I feel okay about coming to school.	You are saying that you feel okay about school.	You should feel happy!
I feel happy when my grandparents visit.	I can hear that you are glad to see your grandparents.	You should feel angry that you have to give up your bedroom for them!
I feel scared when I hear thunder.	You are saying that you are scared of thunder.	Don't be such a baby!

Acquiring Communication Skills

Responding: I Can . . .

Purpose:

to give students information about and practice in responding to the "I" messages they hear

Materials:

◆ none necessary

Activity—Part 1:

Extend what the students have learned about sending and receiving clear messages by talking during your circle time about what to say next. At this grade level, conflicts can be resolved through extending this process. Before tackling an actual conflict, ask two students to act out a guided mediation in a pretend situation. Use the script below as a general outline for your practice mediation.

◆ Pretend that Sally was building a tower out of blocks and that George knocked it down.

> **Teacher:** What is the matter, Sally?
>
> **Sally:** I feel really angry because George knocked down my block tower.
>
> **Teacher:** What did you hear, George?
>
> **George:** Sally is really angry because I knocked down her block tower.
>
> **Teacher:** Is there anything you can do?
>
> **George:** I can help her build it up again.
>
> **Teacher:** What did you hear, Sally?
>
> **Sally:** George said that he would help me build it again.
>
> **Teacher:** Is that all right with you?
>
> **Sally:** Okay. As long as he doesn't knock it down again.
>
> **Teacher:** What do you say, George?
>
> **George:** Okay.
>
> **Teacher:** That was good communication!

◆ Make up some of your own situations and repeat this exchange. Give everybody a chance to practice.

Acquiring Communication Skills

Responding: I Can . . . *(cont.)*

Activity—Part 2:

Encourage the children to apply what they have learned to actual classroom situations. Tell them to come to you immediately if anything goes wrong.

When there is a crisis such as, "Marissa is crying because Chan pulled her hair," stop and try the following:

Teacher: Marissa, when you can stop crying, try to tell me how you feel with an "I" message.

Marissa: I feel angry.

Teacher: When do you feel angry?

Marissa: When Chan pulls my hair!

Teacher: What did you hear, Chan?

And so on. No matter how time-consuming and repetitious this may become, remember that you are giving your students a real tool to use in school, at home, and for the rest of their lives.

Some teachers like to provide a "cooling-off-place," a comfortable spot in the classroom reserved for those who need it. A teddy bear or two make a nice addition to the cooling-off-place. If you have such a place, you could begin the exchange by saying, "Marissa, go to our cooling-off-place and relax until you are calm enough to tell me how you feel with an 'I' message." Often, a hug or an arm around the shoulders of both of the involved students also works well.

Evaluation and Processing:

Discuss the activity . . . Do you like to say how you feel? Do you like to say what you hear? Is it good to have a way to solve problems that come up in the classroom?

Some children may have a harder time than others getting used to this process. Long-term results are the best evaluation of this activity.

Using Techniques for Conflict Resolution

Assertiveness: I Can Stand Up for Myself

Purpose:

to give very young students some acceptable and practical techniques for using assertive behavior

Materials:

- several copies of page 43
- several copies of page 44
- several copies of timing turns signs (page 45)
- several kitchen timers
- "This Is Mine" stickers or buttons (page 46), several for each student
- scissors
- two-sided tape
- crayons

Note: Assertive behavior is hard for adults to learn, so kindergartners may find it very difficult. They, like adults, are more likely to give in (passive behavior) or become angry (aggressive behavior). A workable approach at this grade level is to pick one or two specific situations and then give your students some assertiveness tools and the training to use them. Two such behaviors might be taking turns and protecting personal property.

Activity—Part 1:

At first glance this activity, with all of its signs, looks as if it requires reading. However, if you explain the signs and read them out loud often enough, your students will remember what they say. Model the uses of the signs, wherever you choose to put them, by yourself and with student volunteers. (You might choose to put one of the signs that says "This Is a Taking Turns Activity" next to or above a particularly popular puzzle or over painting easels. Also, post the "Rules for Taking Turns" and the signs that say "One Turn = _____ Minutes" in the same areas.)

During your circle time, tell the students that you are going to show them how to use the signs. First, display them and read them out loud. Orally quiz the children about what the signs say to ensure that they understand. Pass the timers around and let every student have a turn to set one. Then ask two students to demonstrate:

> Have one of the students go to the puzzle table and check the sign that tells how long a turn is. Tell the student to set the timer and begin to play with the puzzle. Have another student go up and start to move the puzzle pieces around. Then say, "Now Susie, you point to the sign and say, 'This is a 'taking turns' activity. Remember the rules.' Let's all remember what they say." (Point to the rules and read them aloud.)

Using Techniques for Conflict Resolution

Assertiveness: I Can Stand Up for Myself *(cont.)*

Continue by saying, "I'm going to pretend Susie's time is up so that we will all have enough time to take turns." (Make the timer ding.) "Now, while Susie cleans up the puzzle area, Johnny will get ready to set the timer. All cleaned up? Okay, Johnny, set the timer and start your turn."

Let Susie and Johnny trade places and repeat the exercise so that Johnny has a chance to make the assertive statement too. Then repeat the whole scenario until everyone has had a chance to role-play.

Continue by saying, "I'm going to put these sets of signs in different places around the room where we have 'taking turns' activities. Remember to say the right words. If you need help, please come and get me. You can also help each other remember what the signs say."

Decide, based on your own situation and group of students, whether or not you want to call attention to the behaviors that are being replaced by this assertive approach. You could say, "Sometimes students think they can't stick up for themselves when someone tries to take an unfair turn. Sometimes students get very angry. These signs and words will help you to stand up for yourself without getting angry."

Activity—Part 2:

Teachers spend a lot of time teaching students to share and then are often upset because they do not respect one another's private possessions. This activity is designed to support the students' right to have their own property rights respected and to remind them to respect the belongings of others.

In your circle, display the "This Is Mine" buttons/stickers. Tell the children that they can use these to tell other people to leave their things alone. Be sure to remind them that they must give other people's things the same respect.

Show them where to find the buttons/stickers and tape and how to put their names on them. Teach the children to act assertively about their belongings. For example, "If someone picks up something that is yours say, 'This is mine. Please look at the sticker.'"

Evaluation and Processing:

The best evaluation of this activity is your own observations of how it is working in lessening both passive and aggressive behaviors in your classroom. Go over the signs and rules with the students from time to time.

Discuss the activities with the children after they have become familiar with the routine. Do they like it? Does it make school a more pleasant place?

Using Techniques for Conflict Resolution

Assertiveness: I Can Stand Up for Myself

This Is a "Taking Turns" Activity

Using Techniques for Conflict Resolution

Assertiveness: I Can Stand Up for Myself

Rules for Taking Turns

1. If someone is using the activity, wait quietly until the timer rings.

2. Give the person time to clean up.

3. When it is your turn, check the sign that tells how many minutes are in a turn.

4. Set the timer.

5. Take your turn and then clean up.

Using Techniques for Conflict Resolution

Assertiveness: I Can Stand Up for Myself

Teacher Directions: Cut out the signs and fold them along the dashed lines. Fill the blanks with the amount of time you would like to permit for the activities. Put a sign and a timer by each "taking turns" activity.

One Turn = _____ Minutes

One Turn = _____ Minutes

Using Techniques for Conflict Resolution

Assertiveness: I Can Stand Up for Myself

Teacher Directions: If you have access to a button-making machine, you can make each student a set of "This Is Mine" buttons. (Have them color the circles and add their names first.) Otherwise, just cut out the circles and have the children color and write their names on them as needed. They can then use two-sided tape to stick the circles to their possessions.

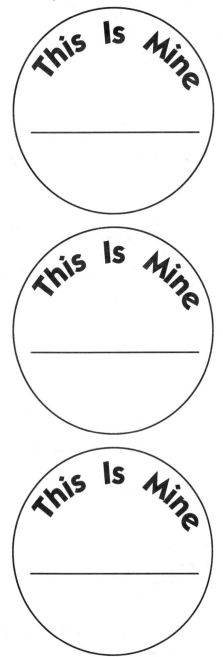 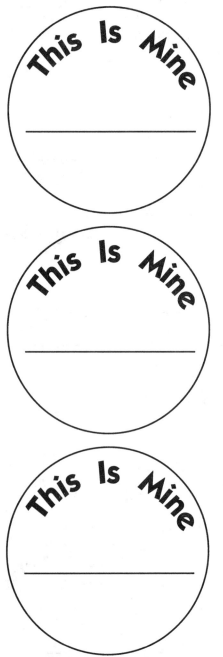

Using Techniques for Conflict Resolution

Negotiation: I Can Think of a Plan

Purpose:
to introduce young students to one of the techniques of negotiation

Materials:
- ◆ chalkboard and chalk
- ◆ copies of planning awards (page 48), one set for every student

Note: In the process of negotiation, two or more sides offer plans and then work their way toward an agreement through a bargaining process. Basic to this approach, of course, is having a plan to offer. Brainstorming is one way of generating plans.

Activity—Part 1:
Tell the children that you have noticed that lately they have really been crowding around the drinking fountain after recess. Explain that this can be dangerous because someone could be pushed and get hurt. It is necessary to think of a way to solve the problem. (Use this situational problem or make up one that is more appropriate for your class.)

Before listening to any ideas, explain that you are going to teach them how to do something called *brainstorming*. Brainstorming is a process in which all ideas are okay. The ideas are all written down without trying to decide if they are good or bad. After we have written down all of our ideas, we will talk about which ones might work the best.

Have your students give ideas while you write them on the chalkboard. They might come up with ideas like these if you are using the drinking fountain problem:

1. Turn off the drinking fountain.
2. Count while people drink.
3. Tap the drinker on the shoulder.
4. Have a drinking fountain monitor.
5. One person at a time gets a drink.
6. Make a nice line.
7. Pushers go to the end of the line.
8. No drinks after recess.

Activity—Part 2:
Discuss the ideas. State the ideal outcome—every person should be able to get a drink without any fuss or too much use of time.

Number six would be the best solution. It would mean that we all could follow the rules without help. Number four would be next best. The monitor could count while people drink, tap the drinker at the end of his or her turn, and send pushers to the end of the line (this answer also includes ideas #2, #3, and #7).

The teacher could let one person at a time get a drink (#5).

Numbers eight and one would be last resorts—things we would have to do if none of the other plans work.

Which plans would you like to try first?

Evaluation and Processing:
After a week, have the students decide if the plan they chose is working. Do they want to keep using it, or is it time to choose another plan? Discuss. Pass out awards.

Using Techniques for Conflict Resolution

Negotiation: I Can Think of a Plan

Teacher Directions: Photocopy these awards onto brightly colored paper. Cut them out and write the students' names on the blank lines.

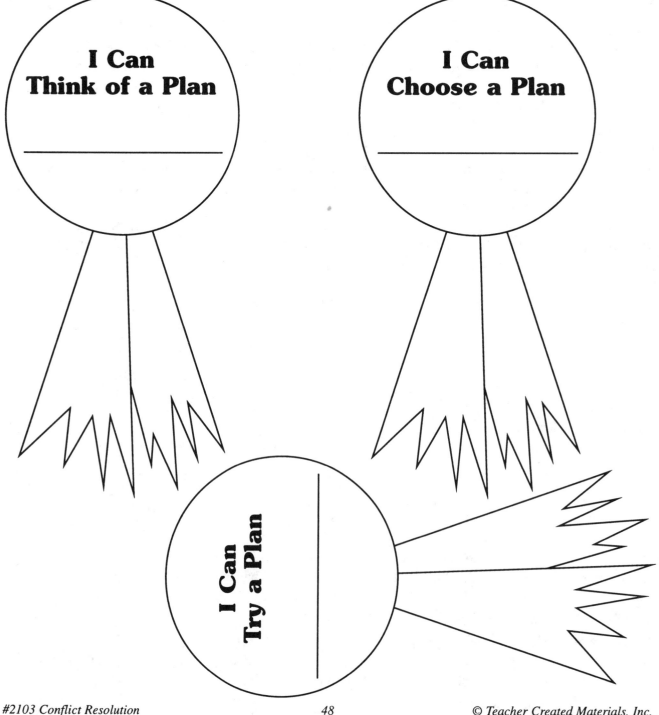

I Can
Think of a Plan
_____

I Can
Choose a Plan
_____

I Can
Try a Plan

Using Techniques for Conflict Resolution

Compromise: I Can Meet You in the Middle

Purpose:

to introduce young students to the idea of compromise

Materials:

◆ an enlarged copy of "Compromise Means . . ." poster (page 50)

Activity—Part 1:

Here is a situation made to order for teaching compromise.

Chan: I want to play with the blocks now by myself!

José: No, I want to play with the blocks now by myself!

Teacher: What is the most important part of playing with the blocks—playing with them now or playing with them by yourself? If playing now is more important, you can play together. If playing by yourself is more important, you can take turns, using the timer.

When you compromise, you meet someone in the middle. You give a little to get a little.

Ask your students what they could do in the following cases.

Student #1: I want the teacher to read *Dr. Seuss's ABCs.*

Student #2: I want him to read *The Very Hungry Caterpillar.*

(Read one book and then the other.)

Student #1: I want to use the blue paint first.

Student #2: I want to use the blue paint first.

(Use another color while you wait to take turns with the blue paint.)

Student #1: I want to play with the red ball.

Student #2: I want to play with the red ball too.

(Play together, take turns with the red ball, or use another ball.)

Activity—Part 2:

Ask the children to tell you when they notice a situation that requires compromising. Have them tell you what each person wants and what their choices are.

Evaluation and Processing:

Discuss the "Compromise Means . . ." poster. Ask your students to explain what it means. (*Two people decide to meet each other half way.*)

Using Techniques for Conflict Resolution

Compromise: I Can Meet You in the Middle

Using Techniques for Conflict Resolution

Mediation: I Can Ask for Help

Purpose:

to introduce young students to the concept of mediation and to let them know that it is okay to ask for help

Materials:

◆ copies of compliment cards (page 52)

Note: In our efforts to teach children not to be tattletales, we often make them feel it is wrong to ask for help from an adult. Older students can be taught to turn to peer mediators for help; however, all children need to know that the teacher is still available to assist in solving problems. If the students have learned to use "I" messages, listen actively, speak assertively, offer plans for solutions, and compromise, there will not be as much of a need for mediation but there will certainly still be some.

Students of all ages, but particularly kindergarten students, need to be protected from bullies. The bully needs to be helped too. More and more research being done in this area shows that bullying is a very serious problem that, left untreated, can result in serious consequences later on in school and in adult life.

Bullies and victims can be identified early by their behaviors and personality characteristics. An excellent and concise overview of both personality types can be found in *Teaching Students to Get Along* by Lee Canter and Katia Petersen (Lee Canter and Associates, 1995).

Both personality types can be helped by activities that build self-esteem.

Activity—Part 1:

During your circle time ask your students to define the word "bully." Do they know any bullies? Has anyone ever bullied them? Discuss.

Activity—Part 2:

Have the children exchange compliments during circle time. Call upon your students one at a time. Ask them to call each other by name and say one nice thing about someone else. ("Mary, I like the picture you painted.") Hand out compliment cards on a regular basis.

Evaluation and Processing:

Tell your students that they are supposed to tell you or another adult when someone is being a bully. This is not tattling. It is something you need to know. If the behavior starts becoming serious, get help right away from your school psychologist or guidance counselor and deal with the situation.

Using Techniques for Conflict Resolution

Mediation: I Can Ask for Help

Teacher Directions: Reproduce these cards and pass them out to your students at the appropriate times.

Developing Respect and Empathy

I Know What You Mean

Purpose:

to let students know that people do not have to agree in order to understand

Materials:

- several enlarged copies of "It's Okay!" banners (page 54)
- *Underwear!* by Mary Elise Monsell, illustrations by Lynn Munsinger (Albert Whitman and Company, 1988)
- copies of page 55, one for each student
- crayons

Activity—Part 1:

Read *Underwear!* to your students during your story time and have a discussion about people who have different ideas about things. *Underwear!* is a story about characters (a zebra, an orangutan, and a buffalo) who have different opinions about underwear. Naturally, a book about underwear is sure to make any kindergartner smile, and this funny little tale is no exception.

Activity—Part 2:

Talk to your students about their likes and dislikes. Ask them about carrots. "Raise your hand if you like carrots. Raise your hand if you do not like carrots. If you do not like carrots, what vegetables do you like?"

Then say: Dan likes carrots. Pham likes celery. It's okay!

(Say it several times and ask the students to chime in with "It's okay!")

Ask the children about pets. Which animals are the best?

Then say: Jodie thinks that dogs are the best pets. Sean thinks that fish are the best. It's okay!

Continue with all the variations you can think of. Put the "It's Okay!" banners up around the room. Use the words quite often. (Jacques likes blocks. Millie likes bikes. It's okay!) Tell the children to draw pictures on page 55 of Bismark before and after he tries wearing underwear.

Evaluation and Processing:

Discuss the activity . . . Is it okay to like different things? Is it okay to think different things? When I like something, does that mean you have to like it too? When I like something, is it okay if you like it too?

Developing Respect and Empathy

I Know What You Mean

Teacher Directions: Enlarge these banners, cut them out, and post them around your classroom.

I Like This. You Like That.

It's Okay!

I Like This. You Like That.

It's Okay!

Developing Respect and Empathy

I Know What You Mean

Directions: Draw a picture of Bismark before he tried wearing underwear and another picture of him after he tried wearing underwear.

BEFORE	**AFTER**

Developing Respect and Empathy

I Know How You Feel

Purpose:

to let students know that they can understand and share other people's feelings

Materials:

◆ *Alexander and The Terrible, Horrible, No Good, Very Bad Day* by Judith Viorst, illustrated by Ray Cruz (Macmillan, 1987)

◆ copies of pages 57–59, one set for each student

◆ crayons

◆ stapler and staples

Activity—Part 1:

Read aloud *Alexander and The Terrible, Horrible, No Good, Very Bad Day* all the way through and then go back and stop to talk about each thing that happened to Alexander. Ask the children if they have ever had a day similar to Alexander's. It is unlikely that any of your students will say that they have had quite as many things go wrong in a day as Alexander, but we all have had days when many things did go wrong. Ask your students how Alexander must have felt. Have them act out Alexander's feelings silently, just using their faces and their bodies.

Activity—Part 2:

Give your students page 57 and show them the word at the bottom—"Morning." Remind them of Alexander's morning. Ask them to each draw something that has happened to them in the morning. Let them brainstorm, if they want to.

Give your students page 58 and show them the word at the bottom—"Afternoon." Remind them of Alexander's afternoon. Ask the children to think of things that have happened to them in the afternoon. Tell them to each draw a picture of one such thing. Let them brainstorm again, if they want to.

Finally, give your students page 59 and show them the word at the bottom—"Evening." Remind them of Alexander's evening experiences. Ask the students to think of something that has happened to them in the evening and draw a picture of it. Let them brainstorm again, if they want to.

You can have the students make covers for their books or just staple the pages together.

Evaluation and Processing:

Discuss the activity . . . How can you tell how people feel? What do their words, the ways they stand, and their facial expressions tell you? Does everybody have the same feelings? How do you know?

Developing Respect and Empathy

I Know How You Feel

Directions: Draw something that happened to you in the morning.

 **Morning**

Developing Respect and Empathy

I Know How You Feel

Directions: Draw something that happened to you in the afternoon.

Afternoon

Developing Respect and Empathy

I Know How You Feel

Directions: Draw something that happened to you in the evening.

Evening

Age-Appropriate Concerns

Moving from Parallel Play to Cooperative Groups

Many conflicts in the classroom, on the playground, and in life in general happen because some children do not know how to cooperate. This is an important skill for children to learn as it will benefit them throughout their entire lives. The remainder of the kindergarten section is devoted to teaching your students the basics of cooperative learning.

Easing into Cooperative Learning

Prepare your students for cooperative learning by conducting whole-class cooperative activities. Whole-class activities are especially conducive to creating a comfortable, safe environment in which students have some knowledge and understanding of one another. It is helpful to ease into the cooperative experience since many beginning students have never had the experience of cooperative interaction.

Parallel Players and Pre-Cooperative Learners

The younger the children are, the less comfortable they will feel in group situations. Most toddlers and preschoolers parallel play. This means that they play near each other at separate tasks. To begin the transition from parallel play to pre-cooperative learning, teachers can focus on teaching children how to get along within the classroom setting. Page 61 offers many activities that support this.

Concepts such as sharing and taking turns are understood by the pre-cooperative learners, and while a pre-cooperative learner may not always feel comfortable trying to share or take turns, these ideas are ones he or she will recognize. Remember, becoming a cooperative learner is a process. Many adults have yet to master the idea in their work situations. Be aware of your students. When they have had enough of a cooperative activity, turn to a less stressful and more autonomous one.

Partner Play

Cooperation is an important component in any classroom. When children cooperate, they have the opportunity to think about and assimilate new ideas.

Use the whole-class activities on page 63 to nurture the cooperative atmosphere within your classroom. Each activity is followed by a suggested partner play. To help ease your children into the concept of cooperative learning, allow them this time to work with one partner only.

Age-Appropriate Concerns

Moving from Parallel Play to Cooperative Groups *(cont.)*

Transitioning to Pre-Cooperative Learning

1. Shoe Hunt/Partner Hunt

Students can use the pattern on page 62 to color two matching shoes. They will write their names on the provided lines. Half of the students can then put one of their shoes into a box, bowl, or other container, and leave their second shoes on their desks. The other half will take turns picking a shoe and matching it to the one on the owner's desk. The students whose shoe was picked will then become that student's partner. Each set of partners will talk together to find out three things about one another. Use the completed shoes for a bulletin board display.

2. Secret Secret

Choose a leader to begin. Have your students stand in a circle. The first person tells the second person a secret. It is then repeated until it reaches the end of the circle and is said aloud. Have the person who began the secret and the person who heard it last compare the differences in the secret. This activity will help your students to understand the importance of listening carefully in their cooperative groups.

3. Walking Through the Neighborhood, I Saw a . . .

Before beginning this activity cut out magazine pictures to represent each letter in the alphabet. Glue each picture onto a piece of cardboard. Write the letter the picture represents on the cardboard. During circle time pass out the pictures, in order, one to each student. Keep the letter "A" for yourself so that you can start the game.

This is a whole-class participation alphabet game. Lead the game with the sentence starter, "I was walking through the neighborhood, and I saw a . . . ." Finish the sentence with the word pictured on your card. For example, "I was walking through the neighborhood and I saw an ant." Continue doing this around the circle until each child has had a turn to share his or her card. If you do not have enough students for the entire alphabet, some children may have to have more than one turn. If you have more students than letters, return to the beginning of the alphabet.

4. Learn to Take Turns

Explore the many ways of taking turns. For example, vote, flip coins, let a neutral party decide, draw straws, draw names, guess a number or a letter, or simply take turns being leader.

Age-Appropriate Concerns

Moving from Parallel Play to Cooperative Groups *(cont.)*

See page 61, "Shoe Hunt/Partner Hunt," for directions.

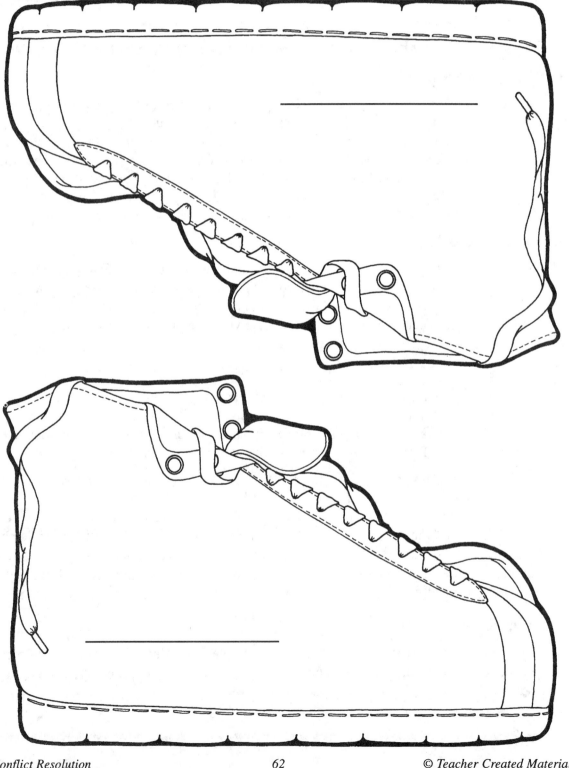

Age-Appropriate Concerns

Moving from Parallel Play to Cooperative Groups *(cont.)*

Whole-class Activities

1. Picture Journal

This activity can be used for individual and partner interaction. Have each child start a picture journal. When any classroom activity ends, have the children draw about the activity. Help them date their entries.

Let the students know that this journal is for them. There is no one right way to do it. It is just for fun. They can look back on it and remember what they did in class and how they felt about it.

Partners: Assign a partner to each child. Partners will discuss their journal entries. This activity will not only help the children to relax in a cooperative learning environment, but it will also build cooperative and communicative skills in a non-threatening way.

2. Rest and Remember

This activity will help the children prepare for or unwind after a classroom activity or special event. Have the children find a place on the floor to lie down. You may wish to dim the classroom lights or play soft music. While the students are resting, ask them to think about the activity that they just completed. Ask them to picture the activity, see it as a mental movie, and decide what they liked and did not like about it. Ask them how they felt—happy, sad, angry, excited, etc. Ask them what they would like to do differently next time they work in their groups. You may then wish to follow up by reading to the students a short, happy poem or story.

Partners: Have the students talk in partners immediately following the "Rest and Remember" exercise, discussing what they liked about the activity they have just completed. This can also be another opportunity to use their picture journals.

3. Letter Home

This activity is helpful in encouraging language and memory skills. It also engenders parental and parent/child participation in your program.

Have the children illustrate what they did in a cooperative learning activity. Let the students take home their picture letters to share with their parents. Have the students return the letters to school and share what their parents thought about the activity and their participation. These letters will also help you to stay in contact with parents consistently, rather than just when there is a problem.

Partners: Have each child view his or her partner's picture letter and make one positive comment or compliment. This activity encourages the students to support each other, and it promotes self-esteem.

First Grade/Second Grade

Developing Self-Concepts

My Name: What Does It Mean?

Purpose:

to give students the opportunity to find out why they were given their names and what their names mean

Materials:

- ◆ a collection of books that give lists of names with their meanings (enough books for the students to share in small groups)
- ◆ copies of letter (page 66), one for each student
- ◆ copies of page 67, one for each student
- ◆ pencils
- ◆ crayons, if desired

Activity—Part 1:

Begin this activity in your large group. Tell your students that they will be learning what their names mean and how they got them. Show them the letter that they will be taking home to their parents. Assure the students that they will be able to complete the activity even if their parents do not fill out the request for information, but it would be good if they could. Pass out the letters to be taken home.

Model the activity by filling out the form on page 67 for yourself. Explain the term "variation." (Bryan is a spelling variation of Brian, for example. Julie is a variation of Julia.) Leave the bottom of the form blank for the time being.

Have the children meet in their small groups and share the name books. Then they may begin filling out their forms. Give assistance and help the groups swap books as needed. Have them leave the bottom part of their forms blank. Collect the forms and save them for Part 2 of the activity.

Activity—Part 2:

After all (or most) of the parent letters have been returned, have the students staple the letters to their forms. In cases where no information has been received from the parents, encourage the students to write what they know about why they were given their names. ("I was named after my grandmother," for example.)

Have each student fill out the last entry on the form individually.

Evaluation and Processing:

Compare and discuss the forms. (Let the students choose whether or not they want to share their last answers.)

Developing Self-Concepts

My Name: What Does It Mean?

Dear Parents:

We are doing a number of activities that will help the students to develop good self-concepts. Since names are very important to people and have something to do with how they feel about themselves, our first activity will center on names. We will be looking at the *actual* meanings of names and their *personal* meanings.

We have gathered together some books that tell the meanings of many names. Just as important, however, are the reasons the names were selected, so we are asking parents to tell us why they chose the names they did for their children. Were they named after a well-loved relative? Were they given a name that has always been in the family? Were they given the name of a character in a book or a movie?

Please fill out the bottom part of this letter and send it back to school with your child.

Sincerely,

I/We chose the name(s)_____because

_____

_____

_____

_____

_____

_____

_____

_____

_____

_____

Developing Self-Concepts

My Name: What Does It Mean?

My first name is _____

It is a variation of _____

My first name means _____

_____

_____

My middle name is _____

It is a variation of _____

My middle name means _____

_____

My parents gave me my names because _____

_____

_____

_____

I like/do not like (circle one) knowing what my name means
because _____

_____

_____

Developing Self-Concepts

How I Look: My Outline

Purpose:

to give students the opportunity to think about how they look and to make life-size paper dolls of themselves

Materials:

- ◆ large sheets of butcher paper
- ◆ marking pens
- ◆ pencils
- ◆ crayons, paints, construction paper, crepe paper, tissue paper, and yarn in a variety of colors
- ◆ remnants and scraps of fabric, if desired
- ◆ scissors and glue

Activity—Part 1:

Tell your students that they will be making life-size paper dolls of themselves. Have two student volunteers demonstrate the process by working as partners to sketch one another's outlines onto sheets of butcher paper. One student should lie down on the paper while the other one draws his or her outline with a pencil. When they are finished, demonstrate how to use a marker to go over the pencil lines.

After the demonstration, have the children divide into partners and sketch one another. When their outlines are complete, students should cut out their own "paper dolls." When everyone has finished, put aside the cutouts for Part 2 of this activity.

Activity—Part 2:

Have your students use the art materials you have gathered together to add features and clothing to their dolls. When the dolls are complete, pin them up around the room with their feet touching the floor so that they become part of the class!

Note: If you are using this activity near Halloween, have the students dress their dolls in the costumes that they plan to wear.

If it is near Back to School Night or Open House, have each child write a greeting for visitors in conversation balloons. Attach the words to the wall next to the dolls.

For Open House, take the dolls off the wall and tape them in sitting positions in the chairs of the students who made them.

Evaluation and Processing:

Discuss the activity . . . What was the easiest part? What was the hardest part? What part did you enjoy the most? If you were to do this again, would you do anything differently?

Developing Self-Concepts

What I Know: Fifteen Things That I Know

Purpose:

to give students the opportunity to think about and share some of the things that they know that are not related to school

Materials:

◆ copies of page 70, one for each student

◆ pencils

Activity—Part 1:

Ask your students to think about the things that they do outside of school—things they do with their parents, brothers and sisters, other relatives, friends, neighbors, coaches, and by themselves. Ask them to think about the hobbies they have, the lessons they take, and the places where they go. Are they really good at or an expert in something that is usually not mentioned in school?

Pass out copies of page 70 and give your students ample time to think while they fill it out. Encourage them to think of enough things to fill in all fifteen of the blanks. Collect the lists and put them aside for Part 2 of this activity.

Activity—Part 2:

Have your students take turns reading their lists aloud to the class. If the students seem particularly interested in an item, make a note. When the sharing has been completed, have the children discuss the different accomplishments that they have heard about.

Ask if any of the students would be willing to teach a skill to the others. If this is a popular idea, help the children set up mini-workshops. Make sign-up sheets to organize the children into workshop groups and then set aside a period for the groups to meet with their "teachers." The students who are not interested in joining a group can read or pursue some other individual activity.

Evaluation and Processing:

Discuss Part 1 of the activity . . . Were you surprised to find out that you know so many things? Was it hard or easy to list fifteen things? Were you surprised at the things the other students listed?

Discuss Part 2 of the activity . . . If you taught a skill to a group, how did that feel? Was it difficult or easy to do? Would you like to do it again? If you attended a group, how did that feel? Did you enjoy it? Would you like to do it again? If you both taught and attended a group, how was that? Which one did you enjoy doing more?

 *Who Am I?*

Developing Self-Concepts

What I Know: Fifteen Things That I Know

Name_____   Date_____

Directions: Think of fifteen things that you know that your classmates may not know about you. Consider your hobbies and activities outside of school.

1. _____
2. _____
3. _____
4. _____
5. _____
6. _____
7. _____
8. _____
9. _____
10. _____
11. _____
12. _____
13. _____
14. _____
15. _____

Developing Self-Concepts

How I Feel: The Best Feeling I Have Ever Had

Purpose:

to give students the opportunity to explore their feelings

Materials:

- ◆ copies of page 72, one for each student
- ◆ pencils

Activity—Part 1:

Ask your students to think about and name some good feelings (happiness, surprise, thankfulness, being needed, being appreciated, and so on). Discuss these feelings. Ask them to think about, but not discuss, how they have experienced these feelings.

Pass out page 72 and give the students ample time to think and write. (If you use the writing process, have them write a rough draft first. Then go through the rest of the process—self-editing, peer-editing, revision, and rewriting—in the course of the next few days.) Collect the finished pieces and put them aside for Part 2 of this activity.

Activity—Part 2:

Remind your students of appropriate listening behavior and talk about giving only positive responses. Then have volunteers take turns reading their pieces aloud to the class. Display the pieces on a bulletin board entitled "Our Best Feelings" for everyone to enjoy.

Evaluation and Processing:

Discuss Part 1 of the activity . . . Was it fun to write about the best feeling you have ever had? Did you experience it all over again when you wrote about it? Did it make you think of other good experiences and other feelings?

Discuss Part 2 of the activity . . . Did you enjoy sharing your story with the rest of the class? Why or why not? Did you enjoy listening to the stories about other people's feelings? Why or why not? Which did you enjoy more, sharing or listening?

Developing Self-Concepts

How I Feel: The Best Feeling I Have Ever Had

Name_____ Date_____

Writing Situation

Feelings can be wonderful! Think about the best feeling you ever had. How did you feel? What made you feel that way? How did you act?

Directions for Writing

Write about the best feeling you have ever had. Try to describe it so that someone else will be able to understand how you felt.

_____

_____

_____

_____

_____

_____

_____

_____

_____

Developing Self-Concepts

My Family: Hanging on My Family Tree

Purpose:

to give students information about and validation of their position in their families

Materials:

◆ copies of page 74, one for each student
◆ pencils

Activity—Part 1:

Sketch a family tree on the chalkboard. Start at the bottom of the board with your own name and branch up to the names of your mother and father and so on.

grandmother	grandfather		grandmother	grandfather

mother		father

my name

Pass out page 74 and tell your students that they will be taking it home so that their families can help them fill it out. Assure them that while some families will have a great deal of information, some will have almost none. This kind of information is very important to some families and of less interest to others. Tell the children that they, or their family helpers, can add more "apples" to their trees as needed.

Activity—Part 2:

When your students return their family trees, encourage them to share what they have learned and then post the trees on a bulletin board.

Evaluation and Processing:

Discuss the activity . . . Was it interesting to fill in your family tree? Did any of the names repeat? (Remind your students of what they learned about how their names were chosen.) How many of the people on their family trees have they met?

Developing Self-Concepts

My Family: Hanging on My Family Tree

Name_____   Date_____

grandmother   grandfather   grandmother   grandfather

mother   father

my name

Developing Self-Concepts

My Friends: What I Want My Friend to Do

Purpose:

to help students become aware of what they want from a friend

Materials:

- copies of page 76, one for each student plus one enlarged copy for demonstration purposes
- pencils
- crayons
- at least two sets of situation cards (pages 77 and 78), cut out and laminated (laminating is optional)

Activity—Part 1:

Discuss with your students the things that are important to them in friends. Encourage them to talk about the things that are important to them. Use the enlarged copy of page 76 to model the activity. Have the students do the activity sheet as you lead them through it on the enlarged copy. Then save the papers for Part 2 of the activity.

Activity—Part 2:

Talk about how all of the things on the activity sheet can be interpreted in more than one way. Divide the class into partners and give each pair a situation card. You and a classroom aide may need to walk around and give assistance to the students in reading the cards. Give each pair a few minutes to talk about their situation and to plan a role-play skit for it.

Have your students take turns presenting their situations and discuss the different solutions that they reached.

Ask for volunteers to write their own situations for things they added to the activity sheet. Have them present these skits to the class and follow up with a discussion.

Evaluation and Processing:

Discuss the activity . . . Was the activity hard or easy? Did you change your mind about any of your requirements for a friend after seeing the situations acted out? Which did you enjoy more—presenting the situation or watching other people? If you did it again, would you do anything differently?

Developing Self-Concepts

My Friends: What I Want My Friend to Do

Name_____ Date_____

Directions: Draw a line from the "friend" to the things that are the most important to you. Add your own ideas on the blank lines. Then use crayons to dress your friend.

Be Nice to Me   **Choose Me in Games**

Stick Up for Me  **Eat Lunch with Me**

Walk Home with Me   **Come Over to Play**

Spend the Night   **Like My Family**

_____   _____

Developing Self-Concepts

My Friends: What I Want My Friend to Do

Be Nice to Me You fell on the way to school and dropped your books all over the street. A group of children made fun of you. What should your friend do?	**Choose Me in Games** You are a really terrible softball player but your friend is a captain and is choosing the team for a big game. What should your friend do?
Stick Up for Me Some students start a fight with you when you and your friend are on the way home. At your school you can get suspended for fighting. What should your friend do?	**Eat Lunch with Me** Your friend has joined a club that meets at lunch one day a week. You want your friend to eat with you. What should your friend do?
Be Nice to Me You went out to recess before your friend and got involved in a game. When your friend came out, he asked you to play with him instead. What should your friend do?	**Choose Me in Games** The teacher has asked all of the team captains to choose different people today. What should your friend do?
Stick Up for Me You found a five dollar bill on the playground. You plan to keep it instead of turning it in. You tell your friend. What should your friend do?	**Eat Lunch with Me** You have already joined a group at a lunch table and saved a seat for your friend. Your friend wants you to move to another table. What should your friend do?

Developing Self-Concepts

My Friends: What I Want My Friend to Do

Walk Home with Me You have to hurry home to get to your karate lesson on time. Your friend needs to return a book to the library on the way home. What should your friend do?	**Come Over to Play** Your friend has played at your house every day this week, and you want your friend to come again today. What should your friend do?
Spend the Night You and your friend both want each other to sleep over. You spent the night at your friend's house the last time. What should your friend do?	**Like My Family** Your little brother is a real pest, but he likes your friend a lot. He wants to spend some time in your room with you and your friend. What should your friend do?
Walk Home with Me Your friend's mother said to come straight home after school. Your house is out of the way, but you do not want to walk home alone. What should your friend do?	**Come Over to Play** You have been playing at your friend's house every day after school. Today, you want to play at your house. What should your friend do?
Spend the Night You and your friend have been planning a sleepover for a week. At the last minute, your friend gets another invitation. What should your friend do?	**Like My Family** Your friend hates pizza. Every time your friend comes over, your mother gets pizza as a "special treat." What should your friend do?

Growing in Social Awareness

Names: Around the World with Names

Purpose:

to help students to learn the names of all their classmates, thus recognizing each other as individuals

Materials:

◆ small rewards (stickers, candies, etc.)

Activity—Part 1:

This activity is a variation of the math game "Around the World" in which one student begins by standing behind the person seated next to him or her. The teacher holds up a flashcard and both students race to give the answer first. If the standing student correctly answers first, he or she moves on to stand behind the next seated person. If the seated student correctly answers first, he or she moves on and the first student takes the vacated seat.

"Around the World with Names" is played in a similar way. One student starts by standing behind the person seated next to him or her. If the standing student can say the name of the seated student, he or she moves on. If not, the seated student gets up and stands behind the next student, and the first student takes the vacated seat. The first student to make it all the way around the room (back to his or her own seat) without a mistake is the winner. Repeat this game at frequent intervals until everyone has been successful in going "Around the World."

Tell the students that you are going to be listening to them as they work. Every time you hear a student call another by his or her name, you will be handing out a small reward.

Activity—Part 2:

In your large group, talk about the importance of knowing names and calling people by them. Ask someone who is a good sport to call you "Teacher" so that you can say, "Were you talking to me, little boy (or little girl)?" This usually gets a chuckle and also gets your point across.

Evaluation and Processing:

Encourage your students to talk about how they feel about knowing everyones' names. Is it a good, grown-up sort of feeling? Are they glad when others call them by their names too? What types of feelings do they have then? Have them try to remember the first day of school when they did not know the names of many of their classmates. Does school feel different now? See if they can describe the difference.

Growing in Social Awareness

Faces: Photo Gallery

Purpose:

to give students the opportunity to enjoy the diversity represented in their class

Materials:

- ◆ bulletin board space
- ◆ baby pictures of all of your students
- ◆ copies of page 81, one for each student (you may need to make double-sided copies of this page if you have more students than there are lines on the ballot)
- ◆ copies of page 82, one for each student
- ◆ a grand prize (maybe a bag of candy or a package of new pencils)

Activity—Part 1:

This activity will encourage the students to really look at each other in order to match the baby pictures to their peers.

Clear a low, easy-to-reach bulletin board space and top it with big letters which spell "Who Am I?" Send home the parent letters (page 82) and put the baby pictures aside as they are received so that your students will not see who handed them to you. When you have them all, put them up on the board after school. Attach a "baby ballot" below or next to each picture.

Give the children a week or so to make their choices. When everyone has voted, post the actual identities next to the pictures and circle the correct votes on each ballot. The person who made the most correct choices wins the grand prize.

Activity—Part 2:

In your large group, ask the person who made the most correct choices to explain his or her strategy. What features were the best clues? Were the choices just lucky guesses? Encourage everyone to discuss how people change as they get older.

Evaluation and Processing:

Was this an interesting activity? Did you enjoy making your guesses? Were you identified by many students or just a few? Was anybody guessed correctly by everyone? Was anybody not identified correctly at all?

Growing in Social Awareness

Faces: Photo Gallery

This is a picture of:	Choice made by:

Growing in Social Awareness

Faces: Photo Gallery

Dear Parents:

We are planning a bulletin board in our classroom on which we will display baby pictures of each of the students. Please pick out a picture to share with us and send it to school by_____.

Please write your child's name and your name on the back of the photograph. All of the pictures will be returned, but if it is your only copy, please get a color photocopy made and send in the copy so that no one will need to worry.

We plan to display the photographs without names and let the other students try to identify them. It should be fun, so do plan to drop in and look at our photo gallery.

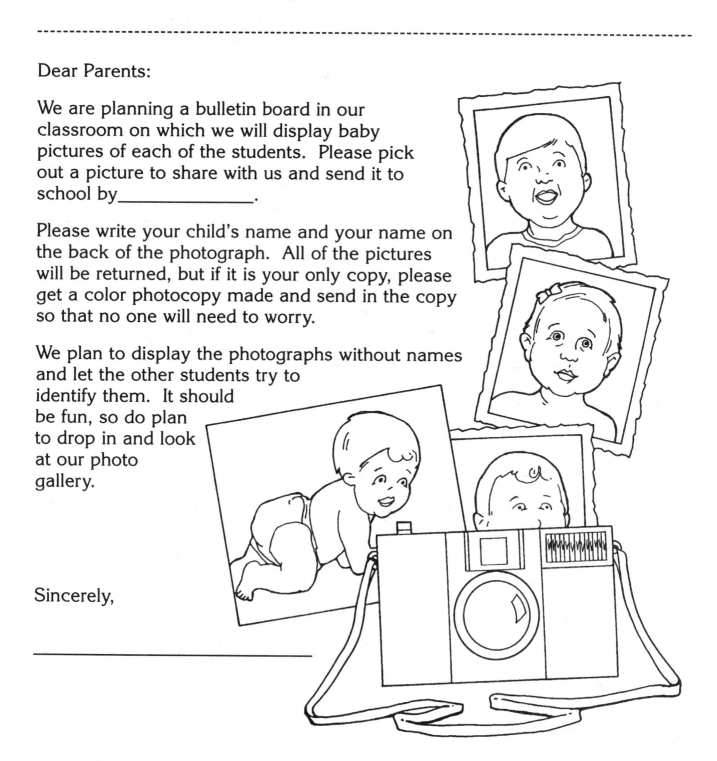

Sincerely,

_____

Growing in Social Awareness

Qualities: Riddles

Purpose:

to give students the opportunity to focus on the positive qualities of their classmates

Materials:

- ◆ copies of page 84, one for each student
- ◆ two copies of your class roster cut into individual name strips and folded in half
- ◆ box, bowl, or hat to draw names from
- ◆ pencils

Activity—Part 1:

Get ready for this activity by writing some riddle clues of your own. Write them about other teachers or school personnel whom the students know. Be sure to tell the students that your clues are about an adult at school. For example:

> I am thinking of someone who is very sweet.
>
> This person always smiles at everyone.
>
> This person never yells or gets cross.
>
> Who is it?
>
> I am thinking of someone who is very patient.
>
> This person always knows everyones' names.
>
> This person is never too busy to help.
>
> Who is it?

Read your riddles to the class and have them guess. Call their attention to the kinds of clues you wrote. They are not physical clues, they never say what the person looks like, and they are all positive. Pass out the activity sheets and tell the students that they will each be drawing the names of two students in your classroom. (If they get duplicates or their own names, they should put the name strips back and draw again.) Have them think about the names they have drawn and write clues that apply to those people. They can use the extra clue form for practice or in case they make a mistake. Be ready to help with words, spelling, etc.

Activity—Part 2:

Collect the clues and read them over so that you can eliminate any that are not positive. Then either read them aloud yourself or pass them back to be read by their authors. Have everyone guess. Cut up the clues and add them to your photo gallery (see the previous lesson) next to the students they describe.

Evaluation and Processing:

Was this an interesting activity? Was it hard to write the clues? Do you feel as if you know your classmates better after thinking about their outstanding qualities?

Growing in Social Awareness

Qualities: Riddles

Name_____ Date_____

I am thinking of someone who is _____

This person always _____

This person never _____

Who is it?

Answer: _____

I am thinking of someone who is _____

This person always _____

This person never _____

Who is it?

Answer: _____

I am thinking of someone who is _____

This person always _____

This person never _____

Who is it?

Answer: _____

Growing in Social Awareness

Similarities: Everybody Plays Games

Purpose:

to use games to help students become aware of and focus on the ways they are similar to children from around the world

Materials:

◆ *Hopscotch Around the World* by Mary D. Lankford (Morrow, 1992)

◆ world map and/or globe

◆ encyclopedias or other reference books

◆ chalk

Activity—Part 1:

Hopscotch Around the World not only gives the history of this ancient game but it also gives the directions for nineteen different versions from around the world.

Read the book aloud to your class, stopping to identify on the map and/or globe the different countries that are represented. Then go back and pick several games that the children in your class might like to try. (You may want to have them vote on this.)

Activity—Part 2:

When you have decided on your games, give your students some facts about the countries where they are played and locate them again on the map and/or globe.

Then take the book, the chalk, and the students and go out to the playground. Try one game at a time but draw the hopscotch pattern two or three times so that no one will have to wait too long for a turn.

Use the book again and again as a resource for your physical education program. Your students will also enjoy having this book available for browsing. Encourage them to play new games. Before you try a new version, go back to the map and/or globe and locate the country where it is played.

Evaluation and Processing:

Discuss the activity . . . Why do you suppose so many people all over the world play hopscotch? How do you think the game traveled from place to place? Do children all over the world enjoy the same things? What makes hopscotch an easy game to play? We played outdoors. Could hopscotch be played indoors? How?

Growing in Social Awareness

Differences: Everybody Plays Games

Purpose:

to use games played in different cultures to help students become aware of and consider the ways that people are different

Materials:

◆ *Musical Games for Children of All Ages* by Esther L. Nelson (Sterling Publishing, 1976)

◆ world map and/or globe

◆ a piano or other musical instrument, if possible

Activity—Part 1:

Although musical games may be a stretch for many teachers, they are particularly valuable to the students with strong musical intelligences. [Musical intelligence has been identified by Howard Gardner (*Frames of Mind: The Theory of Multiple Intelligences*, Basic Books, 1983) as one of the seven basic intelligences or "ways of knowing."] Musical lessons are often overlooked in school. If music is simply not your thing, perhaps an interested parent will come in and accompany you.

Read *Musical Games for Children of All Ages* aloud to your class over a period of several days, stopping to identify on the map and/or globe the different countries that are represented. Since over fifty games are included, this will take a little time. Then go back and choose several games that the children in your class might like to try. (You may want to have them vote on this.)

Activity—Part 2:

This activity can be as simple or as enriched as you want to make it. You can simply read the book and try a few of the games, or you can choose a larger number of them, practice and perfect them, and invite all of the parents to a "Festival of Musical Games."

Evaluation and Processing:

Discuss the activity . . . Which musical game did you like the most? Which one seemed the most unusual and not like any of the games we usually play? What country did it come from? Can you give me any reasons why children in other countries play games that are so different from ours?

If you have a festival, be sure to discuss it too . . . Did you enjoy performing? Was it hard to perform the games in front of other people? If you did it again, would you want to choose the same musical games or different ones?

Growing in Social Awareness

Our Manners: Pass It On

Purpose:

to help students see manners as a way of recognizing the importance of other people, making them feel comfortable, and affecting their moods

Materials:

- ◆ *The Quarreling Book* by Charlotte Zolotow (Harper Trophy, 1982)
- ◆ "School-related Scenario" (page 88)
- ◆ small rewards (stickers, stars, candies, etc.)

Activity—Part 1:

Read *The Quarreling Book* aloud to the class. Discuss the ways in which people have an effect on one another. This book shows a chain reaction within a family. Ask your students how something like this could happen in a classroom. Discuss.

Activity—Part 2:

Talk with the children about the effects they have on one another in school. Have seven students at a time stand in a single-file line. Reread the book, asking the students to act out the situations, assuming the roles of the people in the James family. When everyone has had a turn to do this, read the scenario on page 88 to them. Keep the same teams of seven, or choose new teams, to act out this scenario.

Write additional scenarios of your own to fit the interactions that you have observed in your own classroom.

Be on the lookout for examples of considerate behavior as they occur in your classroom and hand out small rewards on the spot.

Evaluation and Processing:

Discuss the activity . . . Bad moods (and inconsiderate words and actions) can be as catching as the chicken pox. However, good moods, words, and actions can also be catching. Who can tell us what happened in the James family? Who can tell us what happened in the school story? Can these things happen in real life? Do they ever happen in our own classroom?

Growing in Social Awareness

Our Manners: Pass It On

School-related Scenario

Teacher Directions: Line up seven students. As you read the scenario below, allow the children to act out their roles.

Student #1: Bob left his lunch at home. This made him so cross that he kicked Mary's lunch when he sat down at his desk.

Student #2: Mary turned around and knocked a book off her desk. When it fell, it hit José, the boy in the next seat.

Student #3: José was so upset that he was mean to his best friend, Mario.

Student #4: At recess, Mario insulted Jane, a girl from another class.

Student #5: Jane went back to her classroom and kicked over the wastepaper basket, which made the teacher of that class cross.

Student #6: The teacher was in a bad mood and gave that class a big homework assignment.

Student #7: Just then, the principal came in and said, "I've been hearing wonderful things about this class. Keep up the good work!"

Student #6: The teacher laughed and said, "Well, in that case, forget the homework."

Student #5: Jane felt better so she picked up all the paper on the floor.

Student #4: At the next recess, Jane had a nice talk with Mario and they made up.

Student #3: Mario was nice to José when they got back to the classroom.

Student #2: José decided that Mary had not hit him with the book on purpose.

Student #1: Mary asked Bob why he was so upset, and when he told her, she said he could share her lunch.

Acquiring Communication Skills

Sending: I Feel . . .

Purpose:

to give students information about and practice in sending clear messages when they communicate orally

Materials:

- ◆ several enlarged brightly colored copies of classroom banners (pages 91 and 92)
- ◆ several sets of masks (pages 32–36)
- ◆ copies of page 90, one for each student
- ◆ assorted hand puppets

Activity—Part 1:

This activity is designed to help your students express themselves with "I" messages in order to communicate their feelings to others. It can be facilitated through the use of masks and puppets.

Talk about the feelings represented by the masks and ask what other feelings people might have. Brainstorm a list of feelings. (A person can feel upset, nervous, excited, sick, impatient, worried, eager, hopeful, calm, and so on.) Have the children choose four of these words to write on their activity sheets on page 90. Then tell them to design the faces to go with the words they chose.

Use masks as well as hand puppets to express "I" messages. If your students are not familiar with "I" messages, use the activities developed for kindergartners (pages 31–36) to give them a foundation for this kind of communication. Post the classroom banners around the room as reminders to the students to use "I" messages.

Activity—Part 2:

As in the kindergarten lesson, when the students are comfortable with the masks and know the formula for an "I" message, encourage them to use your sharing time to pick up masks and express any feelings they want to: "Stand up or raise your hand if you want to tell us how you are feeling today." Be prepared for painful feelings as well as happy ones. Use this same technique to encourage the students to express their feelings about things that happen in the classroom. Model it yourself to help them understand how to do this: "I feel sad when I see Mary push Sally" or "I feel happy when Joey takes turns."

Evaluation and Processing:

Discuss the activity . . . What part did you like best—the masks or the puppets? Did you enjoy thinking up more feeling words and designing the faces to go with them? Do our banners help you to remember to use "I" messages about your feelings?

Acquiring Communication Skills

Sending: I Feel . . .

Name_____ Date_____

Directions: Think of four ways people can feel. (Do not use happy, sad, okay, angry, surprised, or scared.) Write the four words in the blank lines and draw four faces to match the words.

_____

_____

_____

_____

Acquiring Communication Skills

Sending: I Feel . . .

Teacher Directions: Enlarge these strips onto brightly colored paper to make classroom banners.

I feel happy!

I feel angry!

I feel sad!

Acquiring Communication Skills

Sending: I Feel . . .

Teacher Directions: Enlarge these strips onto brightly colored paper to make classroom banners. Fill in an emotion of your choice on the last banner.

I feel okay!

I feel scared!

I feel

_____!

Acquiring Communication Skills

Receiving: I Hear . . .

Purpose:

to give students information about and practice in listening in order to receive clear oral messages

Materials:

◆ teacher script on page 94

Activity—Part 1:

The first step in active listening is repeating what was said and heard. Your students may have already learned the first step of active listening in kindergarten. If they did, this is a good time to review. Otherwise, teach it now by stressing that they should listen to what is actually said rather than making a judgment about the message.

Remind your students of the "I" messages they have been practicing. Use hand puppets to review. Try using the new feeling words you brainstormed in the last lesson.

The person sending the message should say how he or she feels, using an "I" message.

> **Joan:** "I feel nervous when the teacher calls on me."

> **Pham:** "I feel excited when the ball is thrown to me."

The active listener in this exercise should simply repeat what he or she heard:

> **Rico:** "You are saying that you feel nervous when the teacher calls on you."

> **Ben:** "You are saying that you feel excited when the ball is thrown to you."

During the day send some "I" messages yourself, such as "I feel very happy about the way you picked up!" and then ask the students, "What can you hear?" ("I can hear that you feel happy.")

Activity—Part 2:

Use the script (page 94) on another day. It is like the one used in the kindergarten lesson (pages 37 and 38), but the topics are for grades one and two. Read only the "I" messages aloud. Ask the students to formulate the responses a "good listener" would make. Then read the judgment response. Point out that the good listener lets the person have his or her own feelings. The other response tells the person how he or she *should* feel. Discuss.

Evaluation and Processing:

Watch the students to see if they have internalized the active listening habit. You can see this when they share during a discussion time. ("I feel happy because my mother said I can have a birthday party." The response should be, "You are saying that you feel happy" instead of "Who are you going to invite?")

 *Can We Talk?*

Acquiring Communication Skills

Receiving: I Hear . . .

Teacher Directions: This page is a script for the teacher. Read the "I" messages and have the students formulate their own active listening responses. Then read the "judgment" responses and discuss.

"I" Statement	Active Listening	Judgment
I feel scared when the coach yells.	You are saying that you feel scared when the coach yells.	Just try not to listen!
I feel uncomfortable when I know it is my turn.	I can hear that you feel uncomfortable when it is your turn.	Try holding your breath!
I feel worried when my mother is sick.	You are saying that you feel worried about your mother.	Oh, she'll be okay!
I feel excited that my birthday is soon.	I can hear that you are excited about your birthday.	Are you going to invite the whole class?
I feel good about the test we took.	You are saying that you feel good about the test we took.	That is because you think you are so smart!

Acquiring Communication Skills

Responding: I Can . . .

Purpose:

to give students information about and practice in comprehending and responding to the "I" messages they hear

Materials:

- ◆ copies of page 98, one to use as a teacher script and/or one for each student
- ◆ pencils

Activity—Part 1:

Extend what the students have learned about sending and receiving clear messages by practicing the second step of active listening. The students will now be asked to restate what they hear in their own words. Before tackling an actual conflict, ask two student volunteers to try the following guided mediation in a pretend situation.

Have the students pretend that Ronnie pushed his way ahead of Maria in the lunch line. She is still upset when she comes back to class after lunch.

Teacher: What is the matter, Maria?

Maria: Ronnie is a big bully!

Teacher: Can you tell me how you feel with an "I" message?

Maria: I feel really angry because Ronnie pushed ahead of me in the lunch line.

Teacher: What did you hear, Ronnie?

Ronnie: Maria is really angry because I pushed ahead of her in the lunch line.

Teacher: Can you tell us the same thing in your own words?

Ronnie: I pushed my way through the lunch line to get in front of Maria and she got really mad.

Teacher: Is that right, Maria?

Maria: That's it.

Teacher: Can you do something to make Maria, feel better, Ronnie?

Ronnie: I can say that I'm sorry.

Acquiring Communication Skills

Responding: I Can . . . *(cont.)*

Teacher: Good. Anything else?

Ronnie: I can say I won't do it again.

Teacher: Okay, Maria?

Maria: Okay.

Teacher: That was good communicating!

Repeat this exchange with different fictional situations. Give everybody a chance to practice.

Activity—Part 2:

Try having the students apply what they have learned to real classroom situations. Tell them to come to you immediately if anything goes wrong.

When there is a crisis (such as, Brad left his backpack in the aisle and José tripped over it) stop and try this:

Teacher: José, when you are calm enough, try to tell me how you feel with an "I" message.

José: I feel angry when Brad trips me.

Teacher: What did you hear, Brad?

Brad: José thinks I tripped him on purpose!

Teacher: Just tell us what you heard José say.

Brad: José feels angry when I trip him.

Teacher: Now say that in your own words.

Brad: José is mad at me because he thinks I tripped him.

And so on. No matter how time-consuming and repetitious this may become, remember that you are giving your students a real tool to use in school, at home, and for the rest of their lives.

Acquiring Communication Skills

Responding: I Can . . . *(cont.)*

Some teachers like to provide a cooling-off-place, a comfortable spot in the classroom reserved for those who need it. A teddy bear or two make a nice addition to the cooling-off-place. If you have such a place, you could begin the exchange by saying, "José, go to our cooling-off-place and relax until you are calm enough to tell me how you feel with an 'I' message." Often, a hug or an arm around the shoulders of both of the involved students also works well.

Pass out the activity sheet on page 98 and have your students complete it either orally with you or, depending on their writing abilities, by writing down their answers. If they write their answers, compare and discuss the results.

Evaluation and Processing:

Discuss the activity . . . Do you like to say how you feel? Do you like to say what you hear? Is it good to have a way to solve the problems that come up in the classroom?

Review the two steps of active listening:

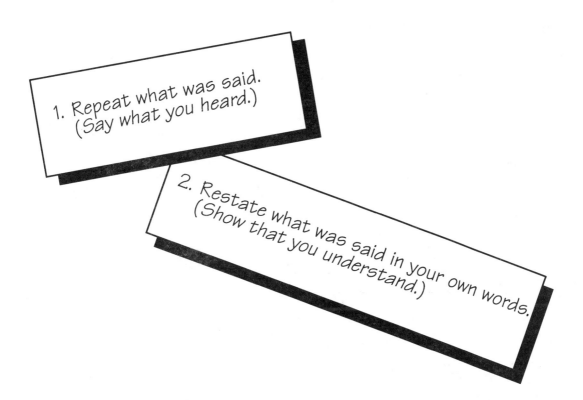

1. Repeat what was said. (Say what you heard.)

2. Restate what was said in your own words. (Show that you understand.)

Some children may have a harder time than others getting used to this process, but long-term results are the best evaluation of this activity.

Acquiring Communication Skills

Responding: I Can . . .

Name_____ Date_____

Directions: Listen while your teacher reads each "I" message. Write down what you hear. Then write the same thing in your own words.

"I" Message	I Hear	I Understand
I feel lonely when my best friend plays with someone else.		
I feel happy when the teacher gives me a compliment.		
I feel angry when someone looks at my paper and copies it.		

Using Techniques for Conflict Resolution

Assertiveness: I Can Stand Up for Myself

Purpose:

to give students information about and practice in making assertive statements

Materials:

- ◆ enlarged copy of "I Am Assertive" poster (page 101)
- ◆ copies of page 102, one for the teacher to use as a script and/or one for each student
- ◆ pencils

Note: Assertive behavior is hard for adults to learn, so first and second graders are apt to find it very difficult. They, like adults, are more likely to give in (passive behavior) or become angry (aggressive behavior).

A workable approach at this grade level is to give your students a formula based on the "I" messages that they have already learned and practiced. Try enlarging and posting the "I Am Assertive" poster in your classroom. Your students may also enjoy using the tools and rules developed in the kindergarten assertiveness lesson (pages 41–46).

Activity—Part 1:

Tell your students . . . Today we are going to learn to be assertive. When you are assertive, you stick up for yourself. You do not give in, and you do not get angry. This sounds hard, but if you can send an "I" message about how you feel, you already know how to do it.

Pretend that you have gone to the classroom library and picked out a book. When you come back and sit down at your desk, the person next to you grabs the book and starts to read it. What would you do?

Would you give in?—Would you not say anything and get another book?

Would you get angry?—Would you grab the book and slam it down on your desk?

Would you be assertive?—Would you say something like "I would like to have my book back. Please get your own."?

Pretend that you are writing a story and that the person next to you keeps looking at your work. What would you do?

Would you give in?—Would you not say anything and pretend that you do not notice?

Would you get angry?—Would you glare at the person and stand a book up to protect your paper?

Would you be assertive?—Would you say something like, "Please do not look at my work. I would appreciate it if you looked at your own paper."?

Using Techniques for Conflict Resolution

Assertiveness: I Can Stand Up for Myself

Pretend that you are on a field trip. The teacher has assigned partners, but your partner keeps wandering away and leaving you alone. What would you do?

Would you give in?—Would you not say anything and join another partner group?

Would you get angry?—Would you yell at your partner "Come back here right now!"?

Would you be assertive?—Would you say "I would like you to stay with me. Please do not wander away again."?

Remember:
◆ An assertive statement is polite, but it is also honest.
◆ An assertive statement shows self-respect and respect for the other person.

Have the students role-play the preceding scenarios and any others that you may want to introduce.

Activity—Part 2:

Depending on the level of your class, use the activity sheet as a script or have pairs of students work together to think of answers for the situations. If the children work in pairs, meet again as a large group when they are finished to compare and discuss the results.

Evaluation and Processing:

This kind of assertive behavior will only work, especially at this grade level, if you have established an environment of high self-esteem, trust, and support in your classroom. Be on the lookout for students who need help with the responses they get after using their assertive statements.

Ask the students to share the results of their assertive behavior . . . Did the other person listen when you spoke assertively? How do you know? What did he or she say? What did he or she do? Were you satisfied with the results? Why or why not?

Using Techniques for Conflict Resolution

Assertiveness: I Can Stand Up for Myself

I Am Assertive!

I would like _____

_____

Please _____

_____

Please _____

_____

I would appreciate it if ____

_____

Using Techniques for Conflict Resolution

Assertiveness: I Can Stand Up for Myself

Your best friend says he or she does not like you anymore and goes off to play with someone else. What would you do?

There are three different ways you could react. Write a description for each way below.

Give In

_____

_____

_____

Get Angry

_____

_____

_____

Be Assertive

_____

_____

_____

Using Techniques for Conflict Resolution

Negotiation: I Can Think of a Plan

Purpose:

to give students information about and practice in a negotiation technique

Materials:

- ◆ copies of page 105, one to be used as a teacher script and/or one for each student
- ◆ pencils

Note: Assertive behavior is only the first step in conflict resolution. If this approach is not met with immediate success, students need to know what to do next. Negotiation, or bargaining, is the next step in this process, and your students will need a great deal of coaching to go on to this new level. In order to bargain in a conflict situation, each side must come up with a plan. Try having your students role-play making plans for the situations you acted out in the preceding activity (pages 99 and 100).

Activity—Part 1:

Tell your students . . . Today we are going to learn what to do if being assertive does not work to resolve certain situations. We are going to talk about *negotiation*. Negotiation is like bargaining. Each side or person in the conflict or problem has to think of a plan.

Remember the first situation we acted out in the last activity? I will read it to you:

> Pretend that you have gone to the classroom library and picked out a book. When you come back and sit down at your desk, the person next to you grabs the book and starts to read it. What would you do?

The *assertive* response was "I would like to have my book back. Please get your own."

If the person who took your book gives it right back to you and goes to get another one, it worked. But pretend that the person says, "No, I won't," and he or she keeps your book.

Now you must come up with a plan. What could you say? (Suggest some responses.)

- ◆ I'll let you read it when I'm finished.
- ◆ Read it first and then give it back.
- ◆ I'll get you another book.
- ◆ I guess I'll have to tell the teacher.

The other person might agree or disagree. What could that person say?

- ◆ I'll let you read it when I'm finished.
- ◆ Okay, I'll read it and give it back.
- ◆ I'll get you another book.
- ◆ Go ahead and tell.

Only one response here shows agreement. Which one? The other answers lead to still another step.

Using Techniques for Conflict Resolution

Negotiation: I Can Think of a Plan *(cont.)*

Remember the second situation? I will read it to you:

> Pretend that you are writing a story and that the person next to you keeps looking at your work. What would you do?

The *assertive* response was "Please don't look at my work. I would appreciate it if you looked at your own paper."

Which responses show agreement?

If the person who has been looking at your paper says "Sorry" and goes back to his or her own paper, it worked. But pretend that the person says "No, I won't" and keeps looking at your paper.

Now you must come with a plan. What could you say? (Get student responses.)

◆ _____   ◆ _____
◆ _____   ◆ _____

The other person might agree or disagree. What could that person say?

◆ _____   ◆ _____
◆ _____   ◆ _____

(Continue with as many situations as you wish.)

Activity—Part 2:

Depending on the writing abilities of your students, use the activity sheet as a script or have partners work together to think of answers for the situation. If the students work in partners, come back together in a large group to compare and discuss the results.

Evaluation and Processing:

Was it hard to think of plan statements? Have you ever done this when talking about a problem with a classmate?

In the next lesson we will talk about compromise. That is the next step.

Using Techniques for Conflict Resolution

Negotiation: I Can Think of a Plan

This was the situation that you thought about on the last activity sheet:

> Your best friend says he or she does not like you anymore and goes off to play with someone else. What would you do?

Your assertive response was probably something like this:

> I still like you and I want to play with you. Please tell me what I can do to make you feel better.

If your friend says, "I still like you. I was just in a bad mood," it worked. But pretend that your friend says "No, I won't" and starts to walk away from you.

Now you must come up with a plan. What could you say?

❄ _____

❄ _____

❄ _____

Your friend might agree or disagree. What might your friend say?

❄ _____

❄ _____

❄ _____

Circle the answer(s) that show agreement.

Using Techniques for Conflict Resolution

Compromise: I Can Meet You in the Middle

Purpose:

to introduce students to the idea of compromise

Materials:

- several enlarged copies of the poster on page 50
- copies of the compromise cards on page 107

Activity—Part 1:

Tell the students . . . Do you remember the first situation we talked about in the last two activities? I will read it, the assertive response, and the plans to you again:

Pretend that you have gone to the classroom library and picked out a book. When you come back and sit down at your desk, the person next to you grabs the book and starts to read it. What would you do? The assertive response was "I would like to have my book back. Please go and get your own."

If the person who took your book gives it right back to you and goes to get another one, it worked. But pretend now that the person says "No, I won't" and he or she keeps your book.

Now you must come up with a plan. What could you say? (Review the responses.)

- I'll let you read it when I'm finished.
- Read it first and then give it back.
- I'll get you another book.
- I guess I'll have to tell the teacher.

The other person might agree or disagree. What could that person say?

- I'll let you read it when I'm finished.
- Okay, I'll read it and give it back.
- I'll get you another book.
- Go ahead and tell.

We said that only one of these responses shows agreement. It was "Okay, I'll read it and give it back" in response to "Read it first and then give it back."

When you compromise, you meet someone half way. You give a little to get a little. Which plans and responses are offers to compromise? Discuss.

Activity—Part 2:

Ask the students to tell you when they notice a classroom situation that needs a compromise. Have them tell you what each person wants and what the choices are.

Evaluation and Processing:

Discuss the poster. Ask the children to explain what it means. (Two people decide to meet each other in the middle.) Hand out the compromise cards when you see compromises in action.

Using Techniques for Conflict Resolution

Compromise: I Can Meet You in the Middle

Using Techniques for Conflict Resolution

Mediation: I Can Ask for Help

Purpose:

to introduce students to the concept of mediation and to let them know that it is okay to ask for help

Materials:

- ◆ copies of mediation requests (page 109)
- ◆ copies of page 110, one for each student
- ◆ scissors
- ◆ pencils
- ◆ instant camera and film

Note: In our efforts to teach children not to be tattletales, we very often make them feel it is wrong to ask for help from an adult. First and second grade students can sometimes be taught the basics of peer mediation; however, all children need to know that the teacher is still available to assist them in solving problems. If the students have learned to use "I" messages, listen actively, speak assertively, offer plans for solutions, and compromise, there will not be as much of a need for mediation but there will certainly still be some.

Also, students of all ages need to be protected from bullies. Bullies need to be helped too. More and more research being done in this area shows that bullying is a very serious problem that, left untreated, can result in serious consequences later on in school and in adult life. Bullies and their victims can be identified early by their behaviors and personality characteristics. An excellent and concise overview of both personality types can be found in *Teaching Students to Get Along* by Lee Canter and Katia Petersen (Lee Canter and Associates, 1995). Both personality types can be helped by activities that build self-esteem.

Activity—Part 1:

Ask your students to define the word "bully." Do they know any bullies? Has anyone ever bullied them? Discuss. Show the children the "mediation requests" and encourage them to use these forms. Have a mediation request box available to put the forms in.

Activity—Part 2:

Build your students' self-esteems with activities that showcase their positive qualities. Choosing a "Student of the Week" helps many students to see both themselves and others as unique and special. Take instant pictures and help the students to fill out the forms (page 110) and post these in a prominent place in the classroom.

Evaluation and Processing:

Discuss your "Student of the Week" program. Ask your students . . . Did you like being chosen? Were your families proud of you? Did you enjoy reading about the other students?

Also, tell the students that they are supposed to tell you or another adult when someone is being a bully. This is not tattling. If bullying seems to be a serious problem for a child, get help right away from your school psychologist or guidance counselor.

Using Techniques for Conflict Resolution

Mediation: I Can Ask for Help

I Need Help!

My name is _____

I have a problem with _____

I Need Help!

My name is _____

I have a problem with _____

I Need Help!

My name is _____

I have a problem with _____

I Need Help!

My name is _____

I have a problem with _____

I Need Help!

My name is _____

I have a problem with _____

Using Techniques for Conflict Resolution

Mediation: I Can Ask for Help

(picture)

_____
Name

My Favorite School Subject: _____

My Favorite Sport: _____

My Favorite Television Show: _____

My Favorite Video Game: _____

My Favorite Book: _____

My Favorite Toy: _____

Developing Respect and Empathy

I Know What You Mean

Purpose:

to let students know that it is perfectly all right to be different

Materials:

◆ *Gramma's Walk* by Anna Grossnickle Hines (Greenwillow Books, 1993)

◆ *Our Granny* by Margaret Wild (Ticknor & Fields, 1994)

◆ copies of page 112, one for each student

◆ pencils

Activity—Part 1:

Read both books, *Gramma's Walk* and *Our Granny*, aloud to your class. Discuss how different the grandmothers are.

> In *Gramma's Walk*, Donnie's grandmother is confined to a wheelchair, but she and Donnie take imaginary walks and talk about what they see, feel, hear, and smell. They share their experiences on the way.

> *Our Granny* is an open-minded look at all kinds of grandmothers. We are introduced through the text, as well as through the illustrations by Julie Vivas, to grandmas of every imaginable shape and size. These interesting ladies are shown going about their varied activities, professions, and lifestyles.

Have a discussion . . . Is it okay to be different? Is one kind of grandmother more "okay" than another kind? What about people who do not know their grandmothers? Is that okay too? Are grandfathers, aunts, uncles, etc., different too?

Activity—Part 2:

Tell your students to each think of a favorite relative to write about. Pass out page 112 and give your students ample time to think and write. (If you use the writing process, have them write a rough draft first. Plan to go through the rest of the process—self-editing, peer editing, revision, rewriting—in the course of the next few days.) Collect the finished pieces and put them aside to share later or post them on a bulletin board for everyone to enjoy.

Evaluation and Processing:

Discuss Part 1 of the activity . . . What did you think of the books? Which one was your favorite? Why? Which grandmother was your favorite? Why?

Discuss Part 2 of the activity . . . About whom did you write? Why is that person special? What makes that person different?

1 **2** >>>>>>>>>>>>>>>>>> *Why Should We Care?*

Developing Respect and Empathy

I Know What You Mean

Name _____ Date_____

Writing Situation

You have listened to the descriptions of many different kinds of grandmothers and we have talked about the fact that it is okay to be different. Think of a favorite relative of your own. What is different about this person that makes him or her special?

Directions for Writing

Write about one of your favorite relatives. Try to describe that person so that the reader will understand how special he or she is.

_____

- -

_____

_____

- -

_____

_____

- -

_____

_____

- -

_____

_____

- -

_____

_____

- -

_____

Developing Respect and Empathy

I Know How You Feel

Purpose:

to let students know that they can understand and share other people's feelings

Materials:

- ◆ *Flower Garden* by Eve Bunting (Harcourt Brace and Company, 1994)
- ◆ copies of pages 114–116, one set for each student
- ◆ crayons

Activity—Part 1:

Read *Flower Garden* to your class.

This is the story of how a father and daughter plan a birthday surprise for their wife and mother. They travel into the city and get the materials for a window garden. The lush illustrations take the reader through a nursery flower shop, on public transportation, and finally home, where the father and daughter create the wonderful surprise. When the mother comes home she finds a lovely window garden in her window.

Discuss the story . . . What feelings are the father and daughter hoping the mother will have when she sees the window box? (surprise, pleasure, joy, love) How can you tell what the mother is feeling when she sees her surprise? Discuss.

Activity—Part 2:

Pass out copies of page 114–116 and ask the children to draw pictures of each of the feelings. The pictures can show people or symbols that stand for the feelings. When the students have finished their drawings, ask them to share them with the class.

Evaluation and Processing:

Discuss the activity . . . How can you tell how people feel? Do their words, facial expressions, or the way they stand tell you anything? Does everyone have the same feelings? How do you know?

Can you change people's feelings? Can you *make* someone feel happy? Can you *help* someone feel happy? When someone you love is sad, how do you feel? When you see that someone you do not know is sad, can you feel that feeling too? (If you feel that your group would be interested, introduce the word *empathy*.)

Why Should We Care?

Developing Respect and Empathy

I Know How You Feel

Name_____

Directions: Draw a picture for each feeling. Do the same on pages 114 and 115.

Love

Dislike

Developing Respect and Empathy

I Know How You Feel

Name_____

Anger

Surprise

①② ≫≫≫≫≫≫≫≫≫≫≫≫≫≫≫ *Why Should We Care?*

Developing Respect and Empathy

I Know How You Feel

Name_____

Happiness

Sadness

Age-Appropriate Concerns

Working as Partners

Purpose:

to give students practice in working as partners

Materials:

- ◆ copies of page 118, one for each student
- ◆ pencils

Activity—Part 1:

Divide the class into partners and give everyone a copy of the interview form. Go over the form with the students as a whole class. Read the questions aloud. Have the partners take turns interviewing each other. Be ready to assist them with reading and spelling words. Next, have the students introduce their partners to the whole class and tell about the facts that they learned about each other during the interviews.

Activity—Part 2:

For Part 2 of this activity you may wish the students to choose new partners or keep the same ones. Have them do all of their work together for one day. They should read aloud to each other, discuss everything, and generally help one another.

On the following day, assign new partners to do the same things.

On the third day, have everyone work individually.

Take a poll . . . How many students liked to work with a partner better than alone? How many students liked to work alone better than with a partner?

Evaluation and Processing:

Discuss the activity . . . If you liked working with a partner, why did you like it? If you liked working alone, why did you like it? Would you like to work with a partner sometimes and alone other times?

Note: The theory of multiple intelligences (Gardner, Howard. *Frames of Mind: The Theory of Multiple Intelligences.* Basic Books, 1983.) indicates that some people are more inclined to work together (interpersonal intelligence) while others like to work alone (intrapersonal intelligence).

Age-Appropriate Concerns

Working as Partners

Partner A _____ Partner B _____

Directions: Write the names of both partners above. Circle the name of the partner asking the questions. Begin the interview.

1. What is your full name?

   _____

2. Where were you born?

   _____

3. When is your birthday?

   _____

4. How many brothers and sisters do you have?

   _____

5. What is your favorite food?

   _____

6. What is your favorite subject in school?

   _____

7. What games do you like to play?

   _____

Age-Appropriate Concerns

Working in Small Groups

Many conflicts in the classroom, on the playground, and in life in general happen because some children do not know how to cooperate. This is an important skill for children to learn as it will benefit them throughout their entire lives. The remainder of the first and second grade section is devoted to teaching your students the basics of working in small groups.

There are four basic components of cooperative learning. These components make the difference between cooperative learning and traditional group activities. Many of the group activities that you have used in the past can be adapted for cooperative learning by adjusting the activities to include the components listed below.

1. **In cooperative learning all of the group members need to work together to accomplish the task**. No one is finished until the whole group is finished. The task or activity needs to be designed so that the members are not each completing their own parts but are working to complete one product together.

2. **Cooperative learning groups should be heterogeneous**. It is helpful to start by organizing groups so that there is a balance of abilities within and among the groups. You may also wish to consider other variables when balancing the groups.

3. **Cooperative learning activities need to be designed so that each student contributes to the group and individual group members can be assessed on their performances**. This can be accomplished by assigning each member a role that is essential to the completion of the task or activity. When input must be gathered from all of the members of the group, no one can go along for a free ride.

4. **Cooperative learning teams need to know the social and the academic objectives of a lesson**. Students need to know what they are expected to learn and how they are supposed to be working together to accomplish the learning. Students need to process or think and talk about how they worked on social skills, as well as to evaluate how well their group worked on accomplishing the academic objective. Social skills are not something that students automatically know; these skills need to be taught.

Age-Appropriate Concerns

Working in Small Groups (cont.)

The teacher's role is quite different during cooperative lessons from what it is during a teacher-directed lesson. The teacher has some important decisions to make prior to the lesson, but when the students are working in cooperative groups, the teacher's role is facilitator instead of trainer. When things are running smoothly, the teacher should circulate and observe how the teams are working.

Teachers may need to intervene in the following situations:

- to get the groups back on target if they are unsure of what to do

- to give immediate feedback to the groups on how they are progressing with the task or activity

- to clarify something or to give further information to the whole class after observing a general difficulty of mastery

- to assist in the development of social skills through praise and group reflection

- to encourage of congratulate the groups on how they are progressing with the task

One caution for teachers is to avoid intervening if a group does not need assistance. Part of collaboration is learning how to discuss what comes next, to examine how the group is doing, and to decide when the group is finished. To successfully progress at this, students need time to work through the different stages and to solve their problems.

Age-Appropriate Concerns

Working in Small Groups *(cont.)*

Teachers often find that using job assignments or roles helps students to know what parts of the task or activity they are responsible for completing. It gives them specific information on what they need to do to help their teams.

Roles that work effectively:

Supplier—gets the materials and supplies for the group

Reporter—reports to the class for the group

Recorder—writes down what the group does, completes the written part of the task or activity, and/or records the group's response during evaluation and processing

Encourager—gives group members praise for their participation and collaboration on the group task or activity

Artist—produces art work

Checker—checks completed work for completeness, neatness, and accuracy

Timekeeper—keeps the group on task and gives time prompts so that the group will complete their tasks on time

Reader—reads directions, text, or looks up information during group work

Clarifier—summarizes or restates the group's responses, conclusions, or premise

The teacher needs to select specific roles for group work, depending on the task or activity. Roles need to be taught and modeled for the class. After a period of experience with cooperative learning, specific roles may not be necessary each time for groups that work well together. In this case, groups will naturally divide up the tasks, with group members doing what they like or are especially capable of doing.

Age-Appropriate Concerns

Working in Small Groups *(cont.)*

Teacher Directions: Make a copy of this page for each student.

> **Once you are in a group there are several things you can do to help accomplish the group's goals.**

Contribute ideas to the group.

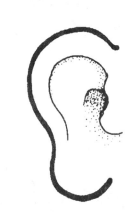

Listen carefully for ideas from others.

Help the group make good decisions.

Cooperate rather than compete.

Solve problems in a calm manner.

Fill in the last box with your own idea.

Third Grade/Fourth Grade

Developing Self-Concepts

My Name: How I Feel About It

Purpose:

to help students internalize and express their feelings about their own names and nicknames

Materials:

- ◆ copies of page 125, one for each student
- ◆ pencils
- ◆ strips of paper (about 8 ½" x 3" or 21.59 cm x 7.62 cm), one for each student with extras available

Activity—Part 1:

Begin this activity with your entire class. Talk about names. Names are important to people. They often have an effect on how people feel about themselves. Nicknames are important too. A good or flattering nickname can increase a person's self-esteem. An unflattering nickname can demolish it.

Have your students complete the activity on page 125 and save the finished papers for Part 2 of the activity.

Activity—Part 2:

Talk about the first part of the activity and let the students share their answers, if they wish to. Then tell them that they will be taking part in an experiment. As a homework assignment, ask everyone to think of a nickname that they would love to have.

Activity—Part 3:

Have the students print their chosen nicknames on strips of paper and stick them to the front of their clothing with double-sided tape. Ask everyone to use these nicknames when talking to each other and be sure to use them yourself. Have the students write their nicknames on their papers. (Make a list, if necessary, so that you do not get their grades mixed up.) Continue the activity for several days. Then talk to your students about how they feel about their new names. Would some people like to keep their new nicknames permanently?

Evaluation and Processing:

Discuss the activity . . . Were you happy or unhappy with your "old" name? Did you feel different with a new name? Did you feel better or worse? What do you want to do now—go back to the "old" name, keep the new one, or choose yet another one? (Try to accommodate each student's wishes. They can wear their final choice in names for a week more until they are all used to the name changes.)

Developing Self-Concepts

My Name: How I Feel About It

Name _____ Date _____

Directions: Answer the following questions about your name and nickname.

1. When I hear my *name*, I feel _____

   _____

   _____

2. When I hear my *name*, I know _____

   _____

   _____

3. When I hear my *name*, I wish _____

   _____

   _____

4. When I hear my *nickname*, I feel _____

   _____

   _____

5. When I hear my *nickname*, I know _____

   _____

   _____

6. When I hear my *nickname*, I wish _____

   _____

   _____

Developing Self-Concepts

Who I Am: I Want to Be Like . . .

Purpose:

to give students the opportunity to think about themselves—and what they would like to change and what they would like to become—and to help students take positive approaches to themselves

Materials:

- ◆ magazine pictures showing positive role models
- ◆ age-appropriate materials about fitness, ambitions, interests, and occupations
- ◆ copies of page 127, one for each student
- ◆ copies of page 128, one for each interested student
- ◆ pencils

Activity—Part 1:

Begin this activity with your entire class. Talk about accomplishments and why people want to achieve certain goals. Pass out copies of page 127 and have your students answer the questions individually. Collect the papers for Part 2 of this activity.

Activity—Part 2:

Talk about the first part of the activity and let volunteers share their answers. Give the students the opportunity to look through the magazine pages and informational materials that you have gathered together. Ask questions such as . . . Did you choose to be like people in any of the magazine pictures? Did you choose a positive role model? Are your feelings about yourself influenced by what your friends, classmates, and family say?

Did any of your students stop with "No" in the first item on the activity sheet? Why do they not want to be like someone else? Are they pleased with themselves? Do they wish to improve in any way?

Activity—Part 3:

Students who really want to change something about themselves can make a plan. Give them copies of page 128. Help and encourage them to set realistic and positive goals for themselves. Give them private and individual help as necessary.

Evaluation and Processing:

Discuss the activity . . . Did you start out wanting to change yourself? How do you feel about it now? Did anything about this activity surprise you?

Developing Self-Concepts

Who I Am: I Want to Be Like . . .

Name _____ Date _____

I want to improve myself. (Circle one answer.)　　　　　Yes　　　　　No

(If you circled "No," give this paper to the teacher. If you circled "Yes," finish the rest of the page.)

I want to be like _____

because _____

_____

_____

_____.

In order to be like _____

I would need to _____

_____

_____.

If I were like _____

my life would be _____

_____

_____

_____

_____.

Developing Self-Concepts

Who I Am: I Want to Be Like . . .

Name _____   Date _____

Directions: Spend some time with your teacher to develop some realistic and positive goals for yourself. Write your goals below.

First Goal

_____

_____

_____

Second Goal

_____

_____

_____

Third Goal

_____

_____

_____

Fourth Goal

_____

_____

_____

Fifth Goal

_____

_____

_____

Developing Self-Concepts

What I Know: Fifteen Things I Would Like to Learn About

Purpose:

to give students the opportunity to think about and express some of the things that they would like to learn about

Materials:

◆ copies of page 130, one for each student
◆ pencils
◆ one large piece of poster paper suitable for making a classroom graph (see the example on page 131)
◆ several copies of page 132
◆ small squares of construction paper (1" x 1" or 2.5 cm x 2.5 cm)
◆ glue stick

Activity—Part 1:

Ask your students to think of some things that they would like to learn about, both at school and outside of school—things they see other people doing, things they read about, things they have seen on television, and so on. Would they like to learn a little about something or become an expert?
Pass out page 130 and give the students ample time to think while they fill it out. Encourage them to think of enough things to fill in all fifteen blanks. Suggest that they might think of ten things to learn in school and five things to learn outside of school. Collect the lists and put them aside for Part 2 of this activity.

Activity—Part 2:

Have the students take turns reading their lists aloud to the class. As interests are mentioned, write them at the bottom of the poster paper and glue one square of paper above each one. If that interest or something closely related to it is mentioned again, add another paper square above it.
When everyone has finished reading the lists, you will probably have many interests with only one or two squares. However, you might have some interests that were listed by many students, as shown by tall columns of squares.

Activity—Part 3:

Choose two or three of the most popular items from the chart and invite experts in those areas to come in to talk to your class.

Evaluation and Processing:

Discuss Part 1 of the activity . . . Were you surprised that you want to know so many things? Was it difficult or easy to list fifteen things?
Discuss Part 2 of the activity . . . Were you surprised at the things the other students listed? Did anyone else list most of the same things that you listed?

Developing Self-Concepts

What I Know: Fifteen Things I Would Like to Learn About

Name_____ Date_____

Directions: Think of fifteen things that you would like to learn more about. These may be things that you would learn in or out of school.

1. _____
2. _____
3. _____
4. _____
5. _____
6. _____
7. _____
8. _____
9. _____
10. _____
11. _____
12. _____
13. _____
14. _____
15. _____

Developing Self-Concepts

What I Know: Fifteen Things I Would Like to Learn About

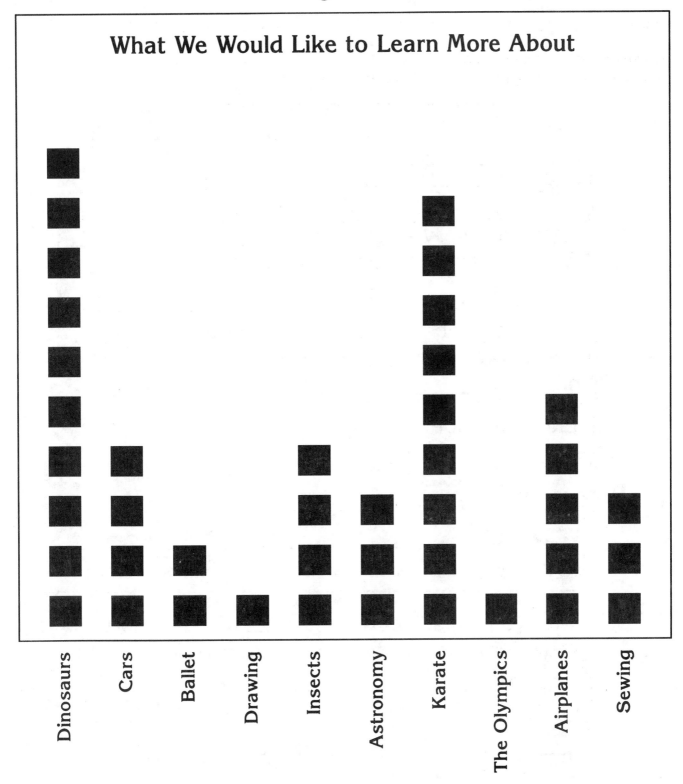

Developing Self-Concepts

What I Know: Fifteen Things I Would Like to Learn About

Dear_____,

We are students in the_____grade at_____School in_____. Our class has been discussing things about which we would like to learn. We are very interested in _____, and we know that you are an expert in this field.

Our teacher suggested that we write to you to find out if you might be willing to talk to our class. If you can come, please contact our teacher,_____, to plan a time.

The phone number of our school is_____.

Here is the address:

_____

_____

We hope you will be able to find the time to do this. Thank you for considering our invitation.

Sincerely,

_____

Developing Self-Concepts

How I Feel: Emotion Definitions

Purpose:

to give students the opportunity to acquaint themselves with words that express the subtleties of emotions and then to use these words to more accurately describe the ways they feel

Materials:

- ◆ copies of page 134, one for each student
- ◆ pencils
- ◆ dictionaries
- ◆ thesauruses

Activity—Part 1:

Tell your students that the ways we feel about things often depends, at least in part, on how we describe our feelings. The more words people know to describe feelings, the better they can think about how they feel. Many dictionaries not only list synonyms for words but also tell about their differences in meaning.

Pass out page 134 and model the activity for the class, using the first word, *love*. Most dictionaries offer synonym paragraphs for words which have many synonyms. These paragraphs explain the subtle differences among the synonyms of the entry word. Look at the example below. It is an abridged version of the synonym paragraph for the word "love" from *Webster's New World Dictionary*.

> *syn*—**love** implies fondness or deep devotion and may apply to various relationships or objects; **affection** suggests warm, tender feelings, usually not as powerful or deep as those implied by love; **attachment** implies connection by ties of affection, attraction, devotion, etc., and may be felt for inanimate things as well as people; **infatuation** implies a foolish or unreasoning passion or affection.

Use the synonym paragraph above to help your students start their activity sheets. Discuss the slight differences in the meanings of the words. (He **loves** his mother and feels **affection** for his friends, but he is really **attached** to his dog.)

Have the students consult dictionaries and thesauruses to complete page 134.

Activity—Part 2:

Let the students share and compare their lists of synonyms and meanings. Ask them to refer to their lists to clarify their feelings when they are speaking and even when they are just thinking to themselves.

Evaluation and Processing:

Discuss Part 1 of the activity . . . Was this part of the activity difficult or easy? Did you learn anything new?

Discuss Part 2 of the activity . . . Have you changed the way you name any of your feelings? If so, what effect has this had on the feelings themselves?

Developing Self-Concepts

How I Feel: Emotion Definitions

Name _____ Date _____

Directions: Write a definition for each of the feelings below. Then write at least three synonyms and their definitions.

love— _____

    1. _____

    2. _____

    3. _____

happiness— _____

    1. _____

    2. _____

    3. _____

fear— _____

    1. _____

    2. _____

    3. _____

surprise— _____

    1. _____

    2. _____

    3. _____

anger— _____

    1. _____

    2. _____

    3. _____

Use the back of this paper to write synonyms for joy and sorrow.

Developing Self-Concepts

My Family: What Makes My Family Special

Purpose:

to give students the opportunity to explore their feelings about their families

Materials:

◆ copies of page 136, one for each student

◆ pencils

Activity—Part 1:

Ask your students to describe a "typical" family. Then ask how many of them actually belong to what some might call a "typical" family. If their families differ in some way from the "typical" family, ask them to think about, but not discuss, how they are different. Remind them that "different" does not mean good or bad—just interesting.

Pass out copies of page 136 and give your students ample time to think and write. If you use the writing process, have them write a rough draft first. Plan to go through the rest of the process—self-editing, peer-editing, revision, rewriting—in the course of the next few days. Collect the finished papers and put them aside for Part 2 of this activity.

Activity—Part 2:

Remind the students of appropriate listening behaviors and talk about giving only positive responses. Then have volunteers take turns reading their pieces aloud to the class. Display the papers on a bulletin board entitled "My Family Is Special" for everyone to enjoy.

Evaluation and Processing:

Discuss Part 1 of the activity . . . Did you enjoy writing about your family and what makes it different? Have you ever thought that being different is wrong?

Discuss Part 2 of the activity . . . Did you enjoy sharing your story with the rest of the class? Why or why not? Did you enjoy listening to the stories of other people's families? Why or why not? Which did you enjoy more, sharing or listening?

Developing Self-Concepts

My Family: What Makes My Family Special

Name_____ Date_____

Writing Situation

Families are made up of people, and people are all different. That makes families different too. There really is no such thing as a "typical" family.

Directions for Writing

Write about what makes your own family different and special. Try to describe your family members so that they seem real to the reader. Use correct grammar.

_____

_____

_____

_____

_____

_____

_____

_____

_____

_____

_____

_____

_____

_____

_____

Developing Self-Concepts

My Friends: Do I Need a Group to Hang Out With?

Purpose:

to give students the opportunity to explore their feelings about themselves in relation to their friends

Materials:

◆ copies of page 138, one for each student

◆ pencils

Activity—Part 1:

Begin this activity with a class discussion. Call your students' attention to the fact that they are in a large group. A group can mean any collection of people gathered together for some purpose or reason. Ask your students to name some different groups (classes, clubs, teams, assemblies, cliques, crowds, gangs, mobs). Draw the discussion to the idea that groups can sometimes be good or sometimes be bad. Outside of the classroom, school groups are often cliques. See if they can define the word "clique" or give them a definition (a small, exclusive circle of people).

Pass out copies of page 138 and give your students ample time to think and write their answers to the questions. Collect the finished papers and put them aside for Part 2 of this activity.

Activity—Part 2:

Poll your students . . . How many students belong to groups? Of those groups, how many are teams? How many are clubs? How many wear distinctive clothing? (Although the students might first think of clothing that identifies gang members, athletic teams and dance groups also wear distinctive clothing.) How many students belong to groups that eat lunch together in a certain place? What do they say to other students who try to sit there, either on purpose or by accident? Is their behavior inclusive or exclusive?

Ask your students to read aloud their answers to question #10. Discuss their answers and compare feelings.

Evaluation and Processing:

Discuss Part 1 of the activity . . . Do you think of yourself as belonging to a group? After filling out the activity sheet, how do you see your group? Should you try to make any changes? If you were to make changes, what would they be?

Discuss Part 2 of the activity . . . Do you depend on your group to feel good about yourself? If so, is that all right with you? Would you call your group a "clique"?

Developing Self-Concepts

My Friends: Do I Need a Group to Hang Out With?

Name_____ Date_____

Directions: Circle your answers.

1. I belong to a group.   Yes   No

   If you circled "No," turn this paper over and write about how you feel about groups and if you would like to be a part of one. If you circled "Yes," finish the rest of this page.

2. The group I belong to includes (takes in) people.   Yes   No

3. The group I belong to excludes (keeps out) people.   Yes   No

4. You can tell who belongs to my group by their clothes.   Yes   No

5. You can tell who belongs to my group by their hair.   Yes   No

6. You can tell who belongs to my group by where we eat lunch.   Yes   No

7. You can tell who belongs to my group by the games we play.   Yes   No

8. My group has a name for itself.   Yes   No

9. Other people have a name for my group.   Yes   No

10. When I am with my group, I feel_____

    _____

    When I am away from my group, I feel _____

    _____

Growing in Social Awareness

Names: A Name Game

Purpose:

to help students learn the names of all of their classmates and to help them recognize each other as individuals

Materials:

♦ copies of page 140, enough copies for each student to write down the needed information for every other student in the class

♦ pencils

Activity—Part 1:

This activity is a variation of a party game. Each student takes his or her "treasure hunt" sheet (page 140) and circulates around the classroom until the blanks are filled in for every other student. (You could model this activity by exchanging information with a classroom aide or a parent helper.)

Give your students some suggestions about what questions to ask to get an interesting fact . . . Do you have brothers and sisters? What is your favorite sport? What is your favorite television show? Do you like video games? Do you have a hobby? What was the best book you ever read? What was the best movie you ever saw?

Activity—Part 2:

This activity can end with Part 1 or you can compile all of the facts collected on all of the forms and make a composite information sheet of each student. Post these composite sheets on a bulletin board and also save them to use in the next two lessons.

Evaluation and Processing:

Discuss the activity . . . What did you like best about this activity? Was there anything you did not like about it? Did you learn anything that you had not known before? Did you learn anything that surprised you? What did you like the most—asking questions or giving answers? If you ever did this activity again with a different group, would you ask the same questions or different ones?

Growing in Social Awareness

Names: A Name Game

Name_____ Date_____

Directions: Fill in the chart below by learning the requested information about every student in your class.

First Name	Last Name	Place of Birth	One Interesting Fact

Growing in Social Awareness

Faces: Photo Opportunities

Purpose:

to give students the opportunity to take pictures of one another for the bulletin board and/or a classroom yearbook/photo album

Materials:

- ◆ camera(s)
- ◆ film
- ◆ bulletin board space
- ◆ a large photo album or scrapbook

Activity—Part 1:

This activity will encourage your students to look at one another in a positive manner as they take pictures for the bulletin board and/or a classroom yearbook.

Because it can get expensive to take and develop pictures, try to make arrangements with your local high school photography class or yearbook staff to develop your film and give you back proof sheets along with your negatives. In this way you will be able to afford to take several pictures of each student and let them choose the ones they like the best.

Draw names for photographic subjects or assign partners who will take pictures of each other. (Partners work the best because they have a vested interest in taking a good picture of the person who will be photographing them.)

Set up a portrait studio in the classroom or encourage your students to look for good backgrounds around your school campus. Allow plenty of time for all of the pictures to be taken. Depending on the number of cameras you have available and the amount of time you want to spend on this each day, it may take a couple of weeks. Some students may be interested enough to complete this activity during lunch hour or other free time.

Activity—Part 2:

When all of the pictures have been taken, developed, and approved of by their subjects, try to have two prints made of each one. One can go up on a classroom bulletin board. The other picture can be mounted in an album/yearbook together with the composite list of interesting facts from the preceding "treasure hunt" activity on page 140 and the results of the activity on pages 142 and 143.

Evaluation and Processing:

Discuss the activity . . . Did you enjoy this activity? Which part was the most enjoyable for you—taking the pictures or having your picture taken? Are you happy with the resulting photographs?

Growing in Social Awareness

Qualities: Our Futures

Purpose:

to give students the opportunity to focus on the positive qualities of their classmates

Materials:

- ◆ copies of page 143, one for each student
- ◆ pencils
- ◆ large photo album or scrapbook from the preceding activity

Activity—Part 1:

This activity will encourage your students to look at one another in a positive manner as they discuss and vote on the "Most likely to . . ." choices.

Pass out the "Most likely to . . ." ballots (page 143) and discuss all of the options. You can either find a person in your class to go with each description on the list or decide on a description to suit each student in your class without necessarily following the list. There is only one rule: If your students make up their own descriptions, they must be stated positively.

You can have open nominations for the descriptions or have everyone vote secretly. When you are finished, you should have a different "Most likely to . . ." description for each student in the class. (If any of the students dislike their descriptions, let them write new ones for themselves.)

Activity—Part 2:

Have one or more students write the descriptions in their best writing (or do it yourself to assure uniformity and legibility) and mount the descriptions below the photographs in the album. Display the album on a classroom table or shelf for your students and visitors to enjoy.

At the end of the school year, the yearbook album can be given to your school library for others to enjoy and for the pictured students to refer to in years to come.

Evaluation and Processing:

Discuss the activity . . . Did you enjoy this activity? Do you agree with all of the choices? Are you happy with your own description? If not, do you want to write another one for yourself?

Growing in Social Awareness

Qualities: Our Futures

Directions: Write the names of your classmates in the blanks. Use the back of this paper to make up more descriptions of your own.

Most likely to *succeed*—_____

Most likely to *become famous*— _____

Most likely to *do well in school*— _____

Most likely to *become a doctor*— _____

Most likely to *get rich*—_____

Most likely to *become a lawyer*— _____

Most likely to *play professional football*— _____

Most likely to *play professional basketball*—_____

Most likely to *play professional baseball*—_____

Most likely to *play professional hockey*— _____

Most likely to *play professional soccer*—_____

Most likely to *become a singer*— _____

Most likely to *become an actor*— _____

Most likely to *become a comedian*—_____

Most likely to *become a writer*— _____

Most likely to *become a dancer*—_____

Most likely to *become a scientist*— _____

Most likely to *become a teacher*— _____

Most likely to *travel*—_____

Most likely to *become a pilot*—_____

Most likely to *get A's all through school*— _____

Growing in Social Awareness

Similarities: Everybody Tells Stories

Purpose:

to help students become aware of and consider the ways in which people are similar through the experiences of stories that are told in different cultures

Materials:

◆ several versions of the Cinderella story (see the list below for suggestions)
◆ an enlarged copy of a chart from page 145
◆ world map and/or globe

Activity—Part 1:

Begin this activity with a class discussion about the story of Cinderella. You may wish to read a basic version of the story, or you may just have the students recap the highlights of the story instead.

Tell your students that they are not the only ones who enjoy the story of Cinderella. There are about 100 versions of the Cinderella story around the world. The most ancient version of the story comes from 9th century China. The story of Cinderella is a treasure shared by many cultures in one way or another.

Activity—Part 2:

Every day read one version of the Cinderella story. Before you begin each story show your students, on a map or a globe, the country from which the story comes. As you read, you may wish to stop at intervals and have the students predict what will happen next. After reading each version of the story, discuss it and fill out part of a story chart. Choose one of the charts on page 145 and compare the stories daily.

The following are suggested versions of the Cinderella story.

◆ *Mufaro's Beautiful Daughters* by John Steptoe. Lothrop, Lee, Shepherd, 1987. (an African folktale)
◆ *The Rough-Face Girl* by Rafe Martin. Putnam, 1992. (an Algonquian Indian folktale)
◆ *The Egyptian Cinderella* by Shirley Climo. HarperCollins, 1992. (an Egyptian version)
◆ *Yeh Shen: A Cinderella Story* retold by Louie Ai-Ling. Putnam, 1988. (a Chinese version)
◆ *Cinderella* by Charles Perrault. Knopf, 1988. (a French tale)
◆ *The Brocaded Slippers and Other Vietnamese Tales* by Lynette Dyer Vuong. HarperCollins, 1992. (a Vietnamese version.)
◆ *Abadeha: The Philippine Cinderella* by Myrna J. De La Paz. Pazific Queen, 1991. (a Philippine version)
◆ *Vasilissa the Beautiful: A Russian Tale* by Elizabeth Winthrop. HarperCollins, 1991. (a Russian tale)
◆ *Tattercoats* by Margaret Greaves. Crown, 1990. (a British version)
◆ *Moss Gown* by William Hooks. Houghton Mifflin, 1990. (an American Southern version)
◆ *Prince Cinders* by Babette Cole. Putnam, 1992. (a version in which Cinderella is a male)

Evaluation and Processing:

Discuss the activity . . . Which version of Cinderella was your favorite and why? Did you realize that you have this story in common with so many people from around the world?

Growing in Social Awareness

Similarities: Everybody Tells Stories

Teacher Directions: Choose either one of the following charts. Enlarge your choice and use it for analyzing (through discussion) the differences and similarities among several versions of Cinderella.

Cinderella Story Chart			
Version			
Beginning Words			
The Magic			
Royal Character			
Evil Character			
Animal Character			
Special Number			
Lesson			
Ending Words			

Cinderella Story Chart			
Cinderella			
Country			
Young Man			
Helpers			
Messenger			
Token			

Growing in Social Awareness

Differences: Everybody Tells Stories

Purpose:

to help students become aware of and consider the ways in which people are different through the experiences of stories that are told in different cultures

Materials:

- *Favorite Tales from Many Lands* by Walter Retan (Grosset and Dunlap, 1989)
- world map and/or globe
- encyclopedias or other reference books
- copies of page 147, one for each student
- pencils

Activity—Part 1:

Read *Favorite Tales From Many Lands* over a period of one or two weeks. There are fourteen stories in the book, so you could read one or two each day. Find the countries that the stories represent on the map and/or globe. Look up and share information in reference books about the countries. Discuss the differences in the stories and ask your students to think about whether or not the stories might have been influenced by the places from which they came.

Pass out copies of page 147 and give the students ample time to think and write. If you use the writing process, have them write a rough draft first. Plan to go through the rest of the process—self-editing, peer-editing, revision, rewriting—in the course of the next few days. Collect the finished papers and put them aside for Part 2 of this activity.

Activity—Part 2:

Remind your students of appropriate listening behaviors and talk about giving only positive responses. Then have them take turns reading their papers aloud to the class. Display the papers on a bulletin board entitled, "Stories from Around the World" for everyone to enjoy.

Evaluation and Processing:

Discuss Part 1 of the activity . . . Did you enjoy the stories? Was it interesting to learn something about the countries from which they came?

Discuss Part 2 of the activity . . . Did you enjoy sharing your story with the rest of the class? Why or why not? Did you enjoy listening to the stories of your classmates? Did anyone pick the same story you picked? Were their ideas like yours or were they very different?

Growing in Social Awareness

Differences: Everybody Tells Stories

Name_____ Date_____

Writing Situation

Recently, you listened to fourteen stories from a variety of cultures. Decide which one you liked the most and think about the country from which it came.

Directions for Writing

Write about why you chose this story. Why is it your favorite? Which country is associated with it? What relationship does the story have to the country? Try to explain your ideas so that they will be clear to the reader. Use correct grammar.

_____

_____

_____

_____

_____

_____

_____

_____

_____

_____

_____

_____

_____

Growing in Social Awareness

Our Manners: *Robert's Rules of Order*

Purpose:

to help students understand that rules for behavior are required, even for groups of adults, in order to assure that everyone gets along

Materials:

◆ encyclopedias or other reference books
◆ copies of page 149, one for each student
◆ pencils

Activity—Part 1:

Define "parliamentary procedure" for your students.
parliamentary: doing something according to the rules and customs of the British Parliament (like Congress in the United States)
procedure: the program that is followed; the way things get done

Tell the students that when a group of people forms an organization or club, they always have to agree to a standard set of rules. Otherwise, it would be difficult to get things done because no one would be able to have a turn to talk.

Many people have written up rules for this purpose. Probably, the best known and most popular set of rules is *Robert's Rules of Order*. Today you are going to have a chance to find out about some of these rules and the man who wrote them.

Pass out page 149 and give your students some time to consult reference books to fill in the information. This might be a good time to visit the library. Students can work on this activity alone or in cooperative groups.

Activity—Part 2:

Have your students read and compare the information they were able to find. Help them fill in any blanks they may have. Discuss the reasons for having these rules.

Evaluation and Processing:

Ask the students to create another name for *Robert's Rules of Order*.

Answers for Page 149:

1. Henry M. Roberts
2. He was a United States Army engineer with the rank of Major.
3. 1876
4. He ran several businesses of his church.
5. Constitution and Bylaws
6. Name, Purpose, Membership, Officers, Committees, Meetings, Amendments

Growing in Social Awareness

Our Manners: *Robert's Rules of Order*

Name_____ Date_____

Directions: Use reference books to find the answers to the following questions.

1. What was the author's full name? _____

2. What was his job?_____

3. In what year did he write his book?_____

4. How did he become interested in this subject? _____

   _____

   _____

5. Before a group becomes a permanent organization or club, it should have two

   things. What are they? _____

6. Most organizations have rules about seven basic subjects. List as many of them as
   you can.

   _____

   _____

   _____

   _____

   _____

   _____

   _____

Acquiring Communication Skills

Sending: I Feel . . .

Purpose:

to give students information about and practice in sending clear messages when they communicate orally, especially during conflict situations

Materials:

- ◆ copies of pages 152 and 153, one set for each student
- ◆ pencils

Activity—Part 1:

This activity is designed to help your students accept the following ideas: Conflict is normal. They have the right to say how they feel and what they want. They will communicate more easily if they learn to express themselves in "I" messages rather than "You" messages.

"You" messages use words that attack and blame. Here are some "You" messages:

- ◆ You always interrupt me and make me forget what I was going to say!
- ◆ You never ask before you borrow something from me!

"I" messages express the feelings of the person who is speaking. To facilitate the use of "I" messages, teach your students to use this formula:

I feel_____when _____   _____.   I want _____   _____.

Have your students practice turning "You" messages into "I" messages. Use the samples above and make up some of your own. Here are some possible "I" messages for the "You" messages given above:

- ◆ I feel frustrated when you interrupt me because it makes me forget what I wanted to say. I want to finish what I am saying without being interrupted.
- ◆ I feel angry when you borrow something of mine without asking. I want to be asked beforehand so that I can decide.

Can We Talk?

Acquiring Communication Skills

Sending: I Feel . . . (cont.)

Activity—Part 2:

When the opportunity arises in your classroom, have your students rephrase their actual "You" messages into "I" messages. It will take a lot of practice for your students to overcome what is probably a habit. Listen for students who are attacking one another with "You" messages like these:

"YOU" MESSAGES	"I" MESSAGE SUBSTITUTES
Why do you always bump into my desk when you go by? You always make me mess up my work.	I get so annoyed when you bump my desk and my work gets messed up. I want you to be more careful.
You promised to remember my book. You never do anything you say you will do.	I feel disappointed because you forgot my book. I want you to do what you say you will do.

After everyone has had ample oral practice, have the students complete page 152 and 153 individually. Then meet as a whole class or in small groups to compare and discuss the results.

Evaluation and Processing:

Discuss the activity . . . Was it hard for you to learn to change "You" messages into "I" messages? Were you in the habit of expressing yourself with "You" messages? Have you tried to use "I" messages on your own? If not, do you plan to? If you have, what kind of reaction did you get? Was the other person more or less cooperative than usual? What was your own reaction? Have you gotten used to saying how you feel?

(Make sure that you model "I" messages constantly. It is not fair to say, "This class is always noisy! You embarrass me in front of the other teachers." Rephrase your message in an "I" message.)

3 **4** ⟫⟫⟫⟫⟫⟫⟫⟫⟫⟫⟫⟫⟫ *Can We Talk?*

Acquiring Communication Skills

Sending: I Feel . . .

Name_____ Date_____

Directions: Write an *"I"* message for each *"You"* message.

1. You never stop talking! You keep me from hearing what the teacher is saying.

I feel_____when _____.

I want _____

_____.

2. You ask me for paper every day. You never have your own supplies.

I feel_____when _____.

I want _____

_____.

3. You always pick your best friends for your team. You never give anyone else a chance.

I feel_____when _____.

I want _____

_____.

>>>>>>>>>>>>>>>>>>>>>>>> *Can We Talk?*

Acquiring Communication Skills

Sending: I Feel . . .

Name_____ Date_____

4. You always say bad things about people. You tell me things that makes me feel uncomfortable.

   I feel_____when _____.

   I want _____

   _____.

5. You don't do your share of the group work. You expect other people to do all of the work.

   I feel_____when _____.

   I want _____

   _____.

6. You never clean your desk. Your stuff is all over the floor.

   I feel_____when _____.

   I want _____

   _____.

Acquiring Communication Skills

Receiving: I Hear . . .

Purpose:

to give students information about, and practice in, active listening in order to enhance the communication process

Materials:

- ◆ copies of page 155, one for each student
- ◆ pencils

Activity—Part 1:

The first step in active listening is repeating what was said. An easy way to teach active listening is simply to reverse the formula for an "I" message.

You feel_____when _____
_____.
You want _____
_____.

You can then add the second step which is rephrasing the information to show that it was understood.

"I" message: I feel scared when you jump out at me like that. I want you to stop it.

Active listening: You feel scared when I jump out at you. You want me to stop it.

Message restated: You want me to stop jumping out at you because it scares you.

Activity—Part 2:

Have your students work in small groups on page 155, "reversing the formula." They can make up their own "I" messages, then write statements of active listening with the reverse formula, and finally restate what they heard in their own words. When everyone has completed the task, get together in a large group and read the "reversing the formula" pages out loud and discuss.

Evaluation and Processing:

Watch the students to see if they have internalized the active listening habit. You can see this in the ways people share in your class. ("I feel happy because my mother said I can have a birthday party." Is the general response "You are saying that you feel happy"? or "Who are you going to invite?")

Acquiring Communication Skills

Receiving: I Hear . . .

Name _____ Date _____

Directions: Make up a conflict situation and express it in the "I" message formula. Then, write what an active listener might hear by reversing the formula. Finally, restate the message. Use additional paper to make up other situations and repeat this process.

"I" Message

I feel_____when _____
_____ .
I want_____
_____ .

Active Listening—Reversed Formula

You feel_____when _____
_____ .
You want _____
_____ .

Restated Message

_____
_____
_____
_____

Acquiring Communication Skills

Responding: I Can . . .

Purpose:

to give students information about, and practice in, using a variety of listening responses

Materials:

◆ one enlarged or overhead transparency copy of the communication chart (page 158)
◆ copies of "Speech Checklists" (page 159), one for each student
◆ copies of page 160, one for each student
◆ pencils

Activity—Part 1:

Give the students the following information . . . There is more than one kind of oral message and more than one style of listening. Sometimes people talk about facts and opinions rather than feelings, and sometimes we are not able to listen actively in the sense of repeating out loud what we hear. Nevertheless, the person sending the message must state it clearly, the person receiving the message must understand it, and there must be some response or feedback to make the communication process work.

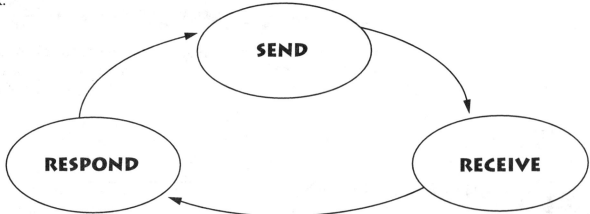

When the sender/speaker is talking about facts and opinions, they need to be organized and delivered in such a way that the receiver/listener can take them in. The receiver/listener (also called the audience) then has the responsibility of trying to understand what is being said. This comprehension must then be communicated back to the speaker. How can this be done?

After you have discussed the above information, ask your students to prepare short talks on any subjects that interest them. This will be most effective if they talk about something that is important to them, something they want the other people in the class to know about too. In giving their talks to the class, they will be "sending" facts and opinions rather than feelings.

Have the students discuss their responsibilities as speakers. They should try to make their talks clear and organized, speak in voices that can be heard, and try to establish eye contact with members of their audience.

Acquiring Communication Skills

Responding: I Can . . . *(cont.)*

Ask your students to discuss their responsibilities as listeners. They should be quiet and attentive, have a positive attitude toward the speaker and the information, and try to take in what is being said. They should be silent, "active listeners," repeating the information to themselves inside their heads.

Before beginning the presentation of the speeches, discuss the ways the audience might respond. The two main audience responses (excluding the clapping at the end of the speech) are eye contact and body language.

Eye contact: This is as much a part of responding as it is of sending. The speaker who is trying to establish eye contact does not have a chance to do so if everyone in the audience is looking at the ceiling or out the window.

Body language: This response is really important. It lets the speaker know that you are interested. Appropriate body language while listening and responding to a speaker can include both posture and gestures. For example, an audience member who leans forward slightly (posture) and nods his or her head (gesture) at important points is giving a positive response.

Ask the students to brainstorm some possible negative responses (leaning back, looking around or at the ceiling, yawning, staring blankly straight ahead, etc.).

Activity—Part 2:

Set aside an afternoon, or an hour on several afternoons, for the presentation of the speeches. After all of the speeches have been presented, have the students fill out the two "Speech Checklists." The top one on page 159 is from the point of view of the speaker, and the bottom one is from the point of view of the audience. Compare and discuss the results.

Activity—Part 3:

Ask your students to consider how the new communication skills they have been learning and discussing could relate to the "I" messages and active listening skills they have been practicing. Pass out the writing prompts (page 160) and give your students ample time to think and write. When they are through, have them share and compare their conclusions.

Evaluation and Processing:

Discuss the activity . . . Which part of this activity did you like best—speaking, listening, learning about a new way to respond, or using the checklists? Which was the easiest? hardest? most fun? If you did this again, is there anything you would do differently?

Acquiring Communication Skills

Responding: I Can . . .

Teacher Directions: Enlarge this chart (or make an overhead transparency copy) and use it during discussions about communication.

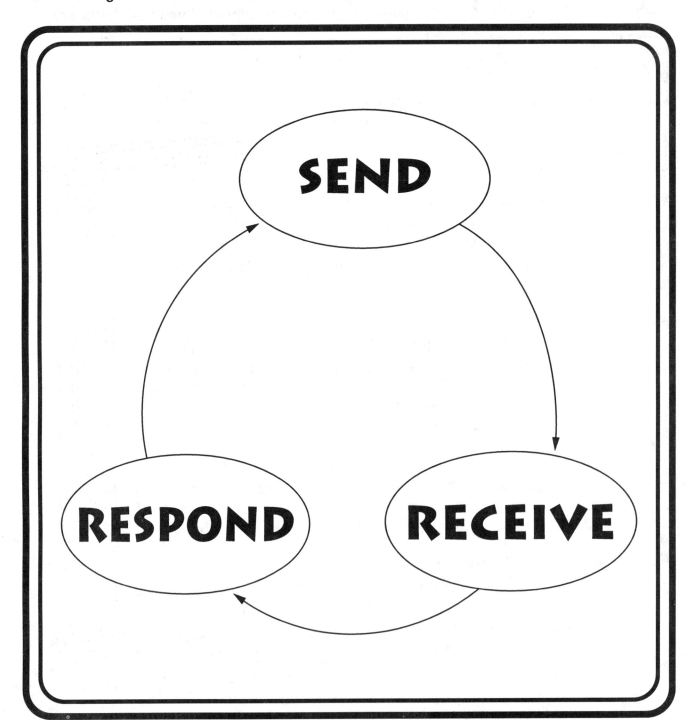

Acquiring Communication Skills

Responding: I Can . . .

Name_____ Date_____

Directions: Analyze your participation in this speech activity. Check off the boxes which pertain to your experience.

When I Was the Speaker:

I felt as if the audience heard me because . . .

☐ . . . no one talked.

☐ . . . they looked interested.

☐ . . . they looked at me.

☐ . . . I was able to make eye contact.

☐ . . . they nodded at the important points.

When I Was the Audience:

I responded by . . .

☐ . . . paying attention.

☐ . . . looking interested.

☐ . . . looking at the speaker.

☐ . . . making eye contact.

☐ . . . nodding at important points.

Acquiring Communication Skills

Responding: I Can . . .

Name_____ Date_____

Writing Situation

You have just finished learning and practicing some new communication skills: talking about facts and opinions, listening quietly and attentively, and responding with eye contact and body language.

Directions for Writing

Write about ways in which these skills apply to what you already know about "I" messages and active listening. Do all of them apply? How can they be used? Be ready to share your ideas with the rest of the class.

_____

_____

_____

_____

_____

_____

_____

_____

_____

_____

_____

_____

_____

_____

COMMUNICATION!

Using Techniques for Conflict Resolution

Assertiveness: I Can Stand Up for Myself

Purpose:

to encourage students to use assertive rather than passive or aggressive behaviors

Materials:

- ◆ copies of page 162, one for each student
- ◆ copies of pages 163 and 164, one set for each student
- ◆ dictionaries
- ◆ pencils

Activity—Part 1:

Tell the students . . . We are going to learn about three types of behaviors—passive, aggressive, and assertive. Very briefly, a *passive* person gives in, an *aggressive* person gets angry, and an *assertive* person stands up for himself or herself.

Many adults go to classes to learn how to be assertive. Some of these adults have found that they are not able to say "no" to requests from other people. Others always react with anger to situations that could be handled assertively instead of aggressively. When you are assertive, you do not give in and you do not get angry. You are in a good position to negotiate and compromise (which are ways of reaching agreements that we will be learning more about).

Here is a situation with examples of the three types of responses:

> A friend of yours is in charge of a committee that collects papers and cans to be recycled. He wants you to join the committee which meets every Saturday morning from 8:00 a.m. until noon. You already have softball practice on Saturdays from 1:00 p.m. until 4:00 p.m. and your mother expects you to do some chores for her too. You really do not want to be on the recycling committee, but your friend is putting a lot of pressure on you, and you know his feelings will be hurt if you refuse.

Passive response: Sure. I'll be there, but I have to leave in time for practice.

Aggressive response: Stop bugging me! I don't want to be on your stupid committee!

Assertive response: I'm sorry, but I can't be there. My Saturdays are already full.

Things to notice:

- ◆ An assertive statement is polite, but it is also honest.
- ◆ An assertive statement shows self-respect, as well as respect for the other person.

Activity—Part 2:

Divide your students into small groups to define the terms on page 162. Then, pass out the situation activity sheets (pages 163 and 164) to the students to discuss and complete. When all of the groups have finished their activity sheets, meet again as a large group to compare and discuss the results.

Evaluation and Processing:

Discuss the activity . . . Did you recognize yourself in any of these situations? Are you usually passive, aggressive, or assertive?

Using Techniques for Conflict Resolution

Assertiveness: I Can Stand Up for Myself

Student _____ Group _____

Directions: Work with your group to define the following terms. You may use dictionaries and/or other reference books.

Dictionary

Passive means _____

_____

_____

_____

_____

Aggressive means _____

_____

_____

_____

_____

_____

Assertive means _____

_____

_____

_____

_____

_____

Using Techniques for Conflict Resolution

Assertiveness: I Can Stand Up for Myself

Student _____ Group _____

Directions: Work with your group to write responses for the following situations. Remember . . .

1. An assertive statement is polite, but it is also honest.

2. An assertive statement shows self-respect, as well as respect for the other person.

Situation One:
Someone you thought was one of your best friends is planning a big overnight party. Everybody is talking about it, and so far you are the only one who has not received an invitation. Your feelings are hurt, and you are also feeling embarrassed about being left out.

Passive response:_____

_____

_____

_____

Aggressive response:_____

_____

_____

_____

Assertive response:_____

_____

_____

_____

Using Techniques for Conflict Resolution

Assertiveness: I Can Stand Up for Myself

Student _____ Group _____

Directions: Work with your group to write responses for the following situations. Remember . . .

1. An assertive statement is polite, but it is also honest.

2. An assertive statement shows self-respect, as well as respect for the other person.

> **Situation Two:**
>
> A teacher wants you to lead a classroom committee that will meet during lunch recess every day for a month. He asked you to do this because you are a good student and your classroom behavior is excellent. You know that the only reason you are able to study hard and maintain your good behavior is because you can look forward to blowing off steam at lunch recess by playing with your friends.

Passive response:_____

_____

_____

_____

Aggressive response: _____

_____

_____

_____

Assertive response:_____

_____

_____

_____

Using Techniques for Conflict Resolution

Negotiation: I Can Think of a Plan

Purpose:

to give students information about how to use negotiation to resolve conflicts

Materials:

- ◆ copies of pages 166 and 167, one set for each student
- ◆ pencils

Activity—Part 1:

Today we are going to learn about negotiation. Negotiation is a bargaining process that helps people on opposite sides of an issue to reach an agreement. The first step in negotiation is for each side to state its demands or tell what it wants. Each side has a plan.

In real life these plans usually contain extra things that the people do not really care about. They are then prepared to give up these things in exchange for things that the other side will give up. (This prepares them for the next step which is compromise.)

The following is a situation with examples of plans offered by two opposite sides.

> Your class is almost evenly divided over the question of extra-credit work. Half of the class wants it to count toward their grades; half the class does not. Your teacher has suggested that each side of the issue should come up with a plan and negotiate a solution.

Plan of the students against extra credit:
- ◆ Grades should be based on required work so that no extra-work is needed for an A grade.
- ◆ Extra credit work could earn bonus points to be applied toward special privileges.
- ◆ Extra credit could be applied to the grades of students getting D's and F's but only to bring those grades up to C's.

Plan of the students for extra credit:
- ◆ No one should be able to get an A grade without doing some extra-credit work.
- ◆ Students should be able to earn special privileges through a system not based on grades.
- ◆ Extra-credit points should count toward the total grades no matter what the students earned on the basic work.

Discuss these plans. Will these opposing sides have any space to work toward a compromise?

Activity—Part 2:

Divide the class into groups and pass out the activity sheets (pages 166 and 167). Tell the students to make up plans for the situations. Then, meet as a large group to compare and discuss the results.

Note: To save paper or to shorten this activity, you may want to give half of the groups one situation and the other half, the other situation.

Evaluation and Processing:

Discuss the activity. Ask students these questions: Were you able to allow room for compromise in your plans? Was it hard or easy?

Using Techniques for Conflict Resolution

Negotiation: I Can Think of a Plan

Student _____ Group _____

Directions: Work with your group to write a plan for each side of the following situation.

> **Situation One:** Your school has a working kitchen and the food is really good, especially breakfast. However, in an effort to cut costs, the school district is considering closing the kitchen and either having food brought in from the district's central kitchen or inviting several fast-food businesses to take part in a food court.

In favor of keeping the school kitchen: _____

_____

_____

_____

In favor of bringing food in from the central district kitchen: _____

_____

_____

_____

In favor of having a fast-food court: _____

_____

_____

_____

Note: Save this completed activity sheet for the next two lessons.

Using Techniques for Conflict Resolution

Negotiation: I Can Think of a Plan

Student _____ Group _____

Directions: Work with your group to write a plan for each side of the following situation.

Situation Two: You want to play in a football league with real uniforms, equipment, and football fields. Your mother wants you to play touch football so that you will not get hurt. Your dad wants you to play golf because it is a sport that you can play for your whole life and also because he is looking forward to having you play with him.

In favor of playing football: _____

_____

_____

_____

In favor of playing touch football: _____

_____

_____

_____

In favor of playing golf: _____

_____

_____

_____

Note: Save this completed activity sheet for the next two lessons.

Using Techniques for Conflict Resolution

Compromise: I Can Meet You in the Middle

Purpose:

to give students information about and practice in reaching compromises

Materials:

- copies of pages 169 and 170, one set for each student
- completed activity sheets from pages 166 and 167
- pencils

Activity—Part 1:

Tell the students . . . Today we are going to learn about *compromise*. When people compromise, they meet each other halfway. Each side may give a little (of what they care the least about) to get a little (of what they care the most about).

Remember the situation about extra-credit work? I will read it and its plans out loud for you again. Think of ways that these two sides could compromise. How could they meet each other halfway? Here is the situation:

> Your class is almost evenly divided over the question of extra-credit work. Half of the class wants it to count toward their grades; half the class does not. Your teacher has suggested that each side of the issue should come up with a plan and negotiate a solution.

Plan of the students against extra credit:

- Grades should be based on required work so that no extra work is needed for an A grade.
- Extra-credit work could earn bonus points to be applied toward special privileges.
- Extra credit could be applied to the grades of students getting D's and F's but only to bring those grades up to C's.

Plan of the students in favor of extra credit:

- No one should be able to get an A grade without doing some extra-credit work.
- Students should be able to earn special privileges through a system not based on grades.
- Extra-credit points should count toward the total grades no matter what the students earned on the basic work.

Can these people reach a compromise based on these plans? Discuss.

Activity—Part 2:

Divide your students into small groups to come up with compromise ideas that might be acceptable to all of the sides. Tell them to use the situations from pages 166 and 167 and to write their compromises on pages 169 and 170. (*Note:* To save paper or to shorten this activity, you may want to give half of the groups one situation and the other half, the other situation.)

Evaluation and Processing:

Discuss the activity . . . Can a compromise ever make everybody completely happy? Were you able to think of ways for the sides in these situations to reach compromises? Was it difficult or easy?

③ ④ ▶▶▶▶▶▶▶▶▶▶▶▶▶▶▶▶▶ *Can We Get Along?*

Using Techniques for Conflict Resolution

Compromise: I Can Meet You in the Middle

Student _____ Group _____

Directions: With your group, look over the plans that you wrote for the following situation. How might these sides reach a compromise? Write your ideas below.

Situation One: Your school has a working kitchen, and the food is really good, especially breakfast. However, in an effort to cut costs, the school district is considering closing the kitchen and either having food brought in from the district's central kitchen or inviting several fast food businesses to take part in a food court.

Compromise Agreement

_____

_____

_____

_____

_____

_____

_____

_____

_____

_____

_____

_____

_____

_____

Using Techniques for Conflict Resolution

Compromise: I Can Meet You in the Middle

Student _____ Group _____

Directions: With your group, look over the plans that you wrote for the following situation. How might these sides reach a compromise? Write your ideas below.

Situation Two: You want to play in a football league with real uniforms, equipment, and football fields. Your mother wants you to play touch football so that you will not get hurt. Your dad wants you to play golf because it is a sport that you can play for your whole life and also because he is looking forward to having you play with him.

Compromise Agreement

_____

_____

_____

_____

_____

_____

_____

_____

_____

_____

_____

_____

Using Techniques for Conflict Resolution

Mediation: I Can Help Others

Purpose:

to introduce students to the idea of peer mediation and provide practice in mediating

Materials:

- ◆ copies of mediation requests (page 109)
- ◆ copies of peer mediation script (page 174), one for each student
- ◆ copies of peer mediator badges (page 175), one badge for each student
- ◆ copies of "Peer Mediator Pledge" (page 176), one for each student
- ◆ safety pins
- ◆ laminating materials
- ◆ pencils

Note: In our efforts to teach students not to be tattletales, we very often make them feel it is wrong to ask for help from an adult. This is just as true in grades three and four as it is in kindergarten through second grade. Although you will probably want your students to learn to be peer mediators, they must still feel assured that the teacher is available to assist in solving problems. If the students have learned to use "I" messages, listen actively, speak assertively, offer plans for solutions, and compromise, there will not be as much need for mediation but there will certainly still be some.

Students of all ages need to be protected from bullies. The bully needs to be helped too. More and more research being done in this area shows that bullying is a very serious problem that, left untreated, can result in serious consequences later in school and in adult life.

Bullies and their victims can be identified early by their behaviors and personality characteristics. An excellent and concise overview of both personality types can be found in *Teaching Students to Get Along* by Lee Canter and Katia Petersen (Lee Canter & Associates, 1995). Both personality types can be helped by activities that build self-esteem.

Activity—Part 1:

Tell the students that they can always ask you for help, but that they are now going to learn how to help each other. Students in many schools are forming groups with names such as Peacemakers, Peace Patrol, SAVE (Students Against Violence Everywhere), and so on. Your plan will begin in your own classroom, but if it is successful and helpful to students, they may want to present it to the school and teach others how to use it. Tell them that they may help any classmate who wants help and that you will make a script available for them to use. Remind them that you will always be available for backup.

Prepare by reviewing some of the earlier lessons about sending information with "I" messages, receiving information with active listening, and responding to information with the appropriate behavior. Run through a variety of situations, letting your students practice being peer mediators. Use the formula on page 172.

Using Techniques for Conflict Resolution

Mediation: I Can Help Others *(cont.)*

Situation:	A visibly upset student (let's call her Dina) comes into the classroom after lunch.
Peer Mediator:	Do you need help, Dina?
Dina:	Frank makes me sick!
Peer Mediator:	Can you tell me what is wrong by using an "I" message?
Dina:	I feel angry and disgusted when Frank calls me names. I want him to stop.
Peer Mediator:	Frank, please come and talk to us. Did you hear Dina?
Frank:	Yeah.
Peer Mediator:	Please use active listening to tell us what Dina said.
Frank:	Dina said she feels angry and disgusted when I call her names, and she wants me to stop.
Peer Mediator:	Now tell us that in your own words.
Frank:	Dina wants me to stop calling her names because it really makes her mad.
Peer Mediator:	Is that right, Dina?
Dina:	Yes.
Peer Mediator:	Can you say anything to make Dina feel better, Frank?
Frank:	Sorry, Dina.
Peer Mediator:	Is there anything that you can do to make Dina feel better?
Frank:	I can stop calling her names.
Peer Mediator:	Do you feel okay about that, Dina?
Dina:	Yes. Thank you.
Peer Mediator:	That was good communication!

Using Techniques for Conflict Resolution

Mediation: I Can Help Others *(cont.)*

Activity—Part 2:

Becoming part of a peer mediation team is a great self-esteem booster for students. You can extend this program to all of your students or have special rules and qualifications for the job. There is something to be said for both approaches. Meeting special requirements is an extra boost for kids; they can be looked up to by others. However, helping others even if you are not perfect yourself can give you added incentive to try. This is entirely up to you, and your decision will probably depend on the makeup of your current group of students and your educational philosophy.

Still another approach is to have the responsibility for being a peer mediator rotate around the classroom, say six students a week. They can wear peer mediator badges (page 175) and take a pledge at the beginning of their week.

Peer Mediator Pledge

I promise to be ready and willing to help anyone who asks for help.

I will be polite and respectful to the people I help.

I will follow the Peer Mediation Script.

I will ask the teacher for help, if necessary.

Also, make sure that your students know that you are always available to help them with their more difficult situations. Show them the mediation requests (page 109) and encourage them to use these forms. Have a mediation request box available to put the forms in.

Evaluation and Processing:

Discuss your peer mediator program. Ask your students . . . Is this helpful? Are the mediators polite and respectful? Is the script useful? Can you suggest any changes we need to make?

Are you happy with the way the mediators are selected. Have you been a peer mediator? If not, would you like to be one? Why?

Using Techniques for Conflict Resolution

Mediation: I Can Help Others

Mediator Directions: In the case of a conflict, use this script to guide a conversation between the two opposing parties. The blank lines are for the students' names and their responses. Highlight your lines ahead of time for easy referencing.

Peer Mediator: Do you need help,_____?
   First Person's Response:_____
_____

Peer Mediator: Can you tell me what is wrong by using an "I" message?
   First Person's Response:_____
_____

*Peer Mediator:*_____, please come and talk to us. Did you hear
_____?
   Second Person's Response:_____
_____

Peer Mediator: Please use active listening to tell us what_____said.
   Second Person's Response:_____
_____

Peer Mediator: Now tell us that in your own words.
   Second Person's Response:_____
_____

Peer Mediator: Is that right,_____?
   First Person's Response:_____
_____

Peer Mediator: Can you say anything to make_____feel better?
   Second Person's Response:_____
_____

Peer Mediator: Is there anything that you can do to
make_____ feel better?
   Second Person's Response:_____
Peer Mediator: Do you feel okay about that,_____?
   First Person's Response:_____
_____

Peer Mediator: That was good communication!

Using Techniques for Conflict Resolution

Mediation: I Can Help Others

Teacher Directions: Write a different student's name on each badge. Cut out and laminate the badges. Use safety pins to attach the badges to clothing.

Using Techniques for Conflict Resolution

Mediation: I Can Help Others

Peer Mediator Pledge

- I promise to be ready and willing to help anyone who asks for help.

- I will be polite and respectful to the people I help.

- I will follow the Peer Mediation Script.

- I will ask the teacher for help, if necessary.

Developing Respect and Empathy

I Know What You Mean

Purpose:

to give students information about understanding what someone else is trying to say

Materials:

- ◆ *Angel Child, Dragon Child* by Maria Michele Surat (Scholastic, 1983)
- ◆ copies of page 178, one for each student
- ◆ copies of page 179, one for each student
- ◆ pencils

Activity—Part 1:

Read the book *Angel Child, Dragon Child* aloud to your class. You can read it all the way through and then discuss it or stop for short discussions as you go. The book is only 35 pages long but there is a lot to discuss, so it may take more than one day. (The important theme for this activity is that Hoa must tell her story so that Raymond can understand it well enough to write it down. The happy ending, in which Hoa's family is reunited, highlights the positive potential of trying to understand what someone else means.)

This book has the added advantage for your students of exploring cultural diversity.

Activity—Part 2:

Divide your class into pairs (Partner A/Partner B) and follow these steps:

1. Each student writes a short account of his or her life on page 178.
2. Partner A tells his or her story to Partner B.
3. Partner B writes the story he or she hears on page 179.
4. Partner B tells his or her story to Partner A.
5. Partner A writes the story he or she hears on page 179.
6. Partners exchange papers and read the matching stories to see if they accurately heard what their partners told them.

Ask pairs of students to read their stories aloud to the class. Get reactions and discuss.

Collect the papers and make your own comparisons. Did your students really hear and understand each other?

Evaluation and Processing:

Discuss the activity . . . When you told your story, did you feel that your partner was listening and accurately recording what you said? Was it difficult to write down your partner's story?

Developing Respect and Empathy

I Know What You Mean

Partner A _____   **Partner B** _____

(Write the names of both partners. Circle the name of the person writing the story on this page.)

Directions: Write a short version of the story of your life.

My Story

_____

_____

_____

_____

_____

_____

_____

_____

_____

_____

_____

_____

_____

_____

_____

Developing Respect and Empathy

I Know What You Mean

Partner A _____ **Partner B** _____

(Write the names of both partners. Circle the name of the person writing the story on this page.)

Directions: Write the story your partner tells you about his or her life.

My Partner's Story

_____

_____

_____

_____

_____

_____

_____

_____

_____

_____

_____

_____

_____

_____

Developing Respect and Empathy

I Know How You Feel

Purpose:

to introduce students to the concept of empathy

Materials:

- ◆ *Sachiko Means Happiness* by Kimiko Sakai (Children's Book Press, 1990)
- ◆ copies of page 181, one for each student
- ◆ pencils

Activity—Part 1:

Begin by reading *Sachiko Means Happiness* aloud to your class. This powerful little book is only 32 pages long, but it gives an excellent look at the feeling of empathy, which some have defined as the most uncomfortable of all human emotions.

In this story Sachiko's dearly loved grandmother has developed Alzheimer's disease. Sometimes she does not even recognize Sachiko, which makes Sachiko feel confused and angry. One evening, thinking that she is a little girl who must find her mother, the grandmother wanders down the sidewalk, crying. Sachiko is overwhelmed with empathy. She knows exactly how her grandmother feels.

Encourage your students to discuss the story and also their own experiences with empathy. Ask your students . . . Have they ever experienced empathy? Is empathy always sad? Can people have empathy for someone who is happy? What about for someone who is excited or scared?

Activity—Part 2:

Have your students define empathy and sympathy (page 181) and discuss the differences between the two feelings.

Discuss how empathy feels. Suggest some ways that a person can show empathy. Ask student volunteers to role-play these situations and have the rest of the class react to them.

Your mother is very upset after finding out that her best friend is very sick.

Your best friend won first prize in a contest that you both entered.

Your dad is worried that he might lose his job.

Your brother is in high school, and he got an "A" on his English test.

Your dad got a big promotion and a raise.

Your mother got the new job she really wanted.

Evaluation and Processing:

Discuss the activity . . . What have you learned about empathy? Is it always easy to empathize?

Developing Respect and Empathy

I Know How You Feel

Name _____   Date _____

Directions: Work with your group to define the following terms and to complete the sentence at the bottom of the page. You may use dictionaries and/or other reference books.

Dictionary

Empathy means _____

_____

_____

_____

_____

Sympathy means _____

_____

_____

_____

_____

The main difference between these two feelings is _____

_____

_____

_____

_____

Age-Appropriate Concerns

Competition and Cooperation

Purpose:

to give students the opportunity to compare the ideas of cooperation and competition and to help them decide when one or the other is appropriate

Materials:

- ◆ copies of page 183, one for each student
- ◆ copies of page 184, one for each student
- ◆ pencils

Activity—Part 1:

Start out by giving your students the activity sheet on page 183. When they have completed it, have them share, compare, and discuss their definitions.

Activity—Part 2:

Let the students work in groups (cooperate) to sort the terms on page 184 into the appropriate columns. Encourage them to make up some of their own items to add to the columns. Ask for the rationale for each placement. See which team put the most items in the correct columns (compete).

Evaluation and Processing:

Ask your students which style they prefer—competition or cooperation. Why? Which one is more exciting? Which one has no winners or losers?

Age-Appropriate Concerns

Competition and Cooperation

Name_____ Date_____

Directions: Work with your group to define the following terms and to complete the sentence at the bottom of the page. You may use dictionaries and/or other reference books.

Dictionary

Competition means_____

_____

_____

_____

_____

Cooperation means_____

_____

_____

_____

_____

The main difference between competition and cooperation is _____

_____

_____

_____

_____

Age-Appropriate Concerns

Competition and Cooperation

Name_____ Date_____

Directions: Put the words from the bottom of the page in the appropriate columns. Add some other words of your own. Think of a good reason for each placement you make.

Competition	Cooperation

football games   football teams   play rehearsal   tennis games

friendship   orchestra   chorus or choir   ice skating

committee work   family life   piloting a plane   racing cars

video games   room cleaning   taking turns   spelling bee

Age-Appropriate Concerns

Rules and Self-Direction: Famous People

Purpose:

to give students the opportunity to think about whether they prefer to follow rules that have been made for them or to exercise self-direction

Materials:

◆ copies of page 186, one for each student

◆ copies of page 187, one for each student

◆ encyclopedias and other reference books and/or library access

◆ pencils

Activity—Part 1:

Discuss with the class some famous people from your social studies text. Ask your students if they think those famous people followed the rules or if they were self-directed. (Opinions will differ on this.) Also ask when it is important to follow the rules and when it is important to be more self-directed.

Make up a list of famous people that you think would be interesting for your students to research for the activity sheet on page 186. Pass out copies of page 186. Let your students each choose three people from the list and give them time to research the names, using the reference books in your classroom or the school library. They should decide whether the three people were self-directed or followed the rules. They will need to give examples to justify their opinions.

Meet as a large group to share and discuss the information and opinions.

Activity—Part 2:

Have each student complete the writing activity on page 187. Encourage them to justify the opinions they assert on this subject. When your students have finished writing, ask them to share what they wrote with the rest of the class. Discuss.

Evaluation and Processing:

Make sure that your students give reasons to back up their opinions in these exercises. Ask them . . . Why do you think that? What makes you think so? Are you generalizing from the information you found in the research you did?

3 ▶ **4** ▶▶▶▶▶▶▶▶▶▶▶▶ *Are We Making Progress?*

Age-Appropriate Concerns

Rules and Self-Direction: Famous People

Name _____ Date _____

Directions: Choose three famous people from history. Do enough research on each person to decide if you feel he or she followed the rules or was self-directed (circle one). Give an example to support each of your opinions.

1. _____ was self-directed.

                                          followed the rules.

    For example: _____

    _____

    _____

    _____

2. _____ was self-directed.

                                            followed the rules.

    For example: _____

    _____

    _____

    _____

3. _____ was self-directed.

                                            followed the rules.

    For example: _____

    _____

    _____

    _____

#2103 Conflict Resolution   186   *© Teacher Created Materials, Inc.*

Age-Appropriate Concerns

Rules and Self-Direction: Famous People

Name_____ Date_____

Directions: You have been considering whether some of the famous people in history followed the rules or were self-directed. Make a generalization on this subject about the people you studied. In general, do you think most of the historical figures followed the rules, or were they self-directed? Decide what you think and write a couple of paragraphs in which you tell why. Use the back of this paper if you need more space.

I think most famous people _____

because _____

_____

_____

_____

_____

_____

_____

_____

_____

_____

_____

_____

_____

_____

Age-Appropriate Concerns

Equal Treatment and Special Circumstances: Fair or Not Fair

Purpose:

to give students the opportunity to compare the ideal of equal treatment with the reality of special circumstances

Materials:

◆ copies of page 189, one for each student

◆ pencils

Activity—Part 1:

Students in the third and fourth grades like everything to be fair. But, as we all must learn, life is not always fair. Discuss the situations described below. Then ask your students to think of other circumstances that might require special, rather than equal, treatment.

◆ There will be a physical fitness test today that you must pass. But your right leg is broken and will be in a cast until next month. Do you think you should get special treatment?

◆ You dropped your glasses on the bus this morning and someone stepped on them. Should you get a bad grade because you cannot read words and numbers?

◆ In order for the game to be really fair, the same rules should apply to everyone. But Zack is in a wheelchair and cannot run. Will you still let him play?

Activity—Part 2

Pass out copies of page 189 and ask the students to complete it. When all of the students have finished this assignment, ask for volunteers to read their papers aloud to the rest of the class. Discuss.

Evaluation and Processing:

This can be a delicate topic if there are students in your class who are sensitive about having some special circumstances of their own. You may want to skip this, only do part of it, or use the opportunity to shed some light on a dark area.

Age-Appropriate Concerns

Equal Treatment and Special Circumstances: Fair or Not Fair

Name _____ Date _____

Directions: There are times when equal treatment would not be fair to the people involved. Tell about a time when special circumstances would require special treatment. Make up a situation or describe something from your own experience. Use the back of this paper if you need more writing space.

_____

_____

_____

_____

_____

_____

_____

_____

_____

_____

_____

_____

_____

_____

_____

_____

Age-Appropriate Concerns

Justice and Compassion

Purpose:

to acquaint students with the necessity for tempering justice with compassion

Materials:

- *Lila on the Landing* by Sue Alexander (Clarion, 1987)
- copies of page 191, one for each student
- pencils

Activity—Part 1:

Take two or three days to read and discuss *Lila on the Landing* with your class.

Ask your class, "If justice had prevailed in this story, would Lila have invited Alan to stay and play after the way he had treated her?"

Activity—Part 2:

Have the students define and compare *justice* and *compassion* by completing page 191. Let them share their definitions and other answers with the class.

Evaluation and Processing:

The question of when it is appropriate to be just and when it is appropriate to be compassionate is a pretty philosophical question for third and fourth graders. However, you may be surprised at their grasp of these ideas. It will, at least, familiarize them with the terms and expose them to the concepts.

Age-Appropriate Concerns

Justice and Compassion

Name _____   Date _____

Directions: Work with your group to define the following terms and to answer the questions. You may use dictionaries and/or other reference books.

Dictionary

Justice means _____

_____

_____

_____

Compassion means _____

_____

_____

_____

The main difference between justice and compassion is _____

_____

_____

_____

Is it always necessary or wise to be compassionate? _____

_____

_____

Thematic Teaching

Thematic teaching is an instructional method that centers the entire curriculum around a theme. For the duration of a thematic unit, a classroom's literature, content area lessons, and activities all relate and reinforce the chosen topic. Current research into the way the brain acquires knowledge shows that students learn and retain more by practicing and applying their skills in meaningful contexts. When new knowledge can be linked to prior experience and connections between pieces of information are apparent, comprehension is enhanced. Higher level thinking skills which are needed to analyze, synthesize, and evaluate the knowledge can be invoked. In a thematic classroom both teachers and students will be freed from a day that is broken into unrelated segments of isolated drill and practice on skills for which there is no obvious real-life application.

Thematic teaching is a natural technique for the classroom where all modes of communication are utilized and literature is key. Units with activities that extend across the curriculum can be developed from the items found in the literature being used or from the subjects being taught. In traditional classrooms, social studies and science topics, for example, can be developed into thematic units with the addition of appropriate literature and activities from other curriculum areas. Bulletin boards, decorations, and hands-on apparatus related to the theme set the atmosphere of the classroom. Writing, research, cooperative learning projects, community involvement, and authentic assessment procedures are planned by students and teacher together. All elements are drawn together like the threads of a spider web, ultimately capturing student interest and encouraging success.

On the following pages is a complete thematic unit about friendship for primary students. You may wish to use this unit as an introduction to teaching about conflict resolution or as a wrap-up to the conflict resolution lessons.

A Thematic Unit on Friendship

Level:

Primary

Literature Selection:

Friends by Helme Heine (S & S Childrens, 1986)

Summary:

Friends are so much fun to be with! In this delightful story of friendship you will meet Charlie Rooster, Johnny Mouse, and Percy, the pig. They wake up the barnyard, go for a morning bike ride, play hide-and-seek, pretend to be pirates, go fishing, pig out (no pun intended) on cherries, and pledge to be friends forever!

Teacher Preparation:

The book *Friends* addresses the fact that we all need friends. Its whimsical look at friendship shows us that cooperation is a great way to get things accomplished. Collect and display books on friendship. Let your students take turns reading them to their friends in class or checking them out to share with their friends at home.

Create a friendship bulletin board. Back a bulletin board with any darkly-colored construction paper. Cut each letter in the word FRIENDSHIP out of 24" x 36" (60.96 cm x 91.44 cm) contrasting construction paper. Let your students draw pictures of their friends or bring in photographs and staple these to the letters.

Overview of Activities

Setting the Stage: *Friends*

What is a friend? Brainstorm with your students about what they believe are the qualities of a friend. Encourage them to recognize that classmates, family members, people in their neighborhoods, and even animals can be their friends! Write their ideas on butcher paper.

Make a graph of your students' friends. Give each student two square-shaped sticky notepad sheets. Have them each draw the faces of two of their friends. Draw a graph on butcher paper. Draw three columns on the graph and label them MALE, FEMALE, and ANIMAL. Have the students come up and place their sticky note sheets in the appropriate columns. When all of the students have placed their sheets, study the results. Encourage mathematical comparisons; for example, "More students in our class have friends that are girls than friends that are boys."

Enjoying the Book: *Friends*

When reading the story, *Friends,* explain to your students that you want them to notice how each of the three characters shows he is a friend, by using the text and the picture clues. After the initial reading, list their observations on paper "headed" by the animals' faces (patterns are on page 195). Post their findings in the classroom with the title "Friendly Observations."

Have the children act out the story as a play or use the faces on page 195 as stick puppets to retell it. To make stick puppets, copy the faces onto tagboard and have the students color them appropriately. Cut out the faces and staple them to tongue depressors or craft sticks.

Cooperation is very important in friendship and in working together in the classroom. Discuss how the three animals cooperated to make the bicycle work. Divide the class into cooperative teams of three or four. Have each team draw a picture and write about a machine or vehicle that they could operate by working together. Have each team share their picture and sentences. Display the cooperative works of art and sentences on a bulletin board.

Overview of Activities *(cont.)*

Friends' Faces

See suggested activities page 194.

Faces can be used as stick puppets.

Overview of Activities *(cont.)*

Extending the Book: *Friends*

Friends Help Each Other!

Ask the students to think of times when they have helped their friends. Give an example of a time that you helped a friend. Ask the students to give examples of how the animals in the story helped each other. List their replies on butcher paper.

1. Johnny Mouse and Percy Pig helped Charlie Rooster wake up the barnyard animals.

2. To ride the bike, Charlie Rooster steered while Percy and Johnny Mouse pedaled.

3. Johnny Mouse steered the boat while Charlie Rooster helped it to sail, and Percy covered up the hole in the bottom of the boat with his body.

4. Percy held Johnny Mouse while the mouse used his tail to go fishing, and Charlie Rooster took care of the worms in his beak.

5. They all helped each other to reach the cherries by standing on each other's shoulders.

6. Johnny Mouse and Percy helped Charlie Rooster's anger by giving him the cherry pits.

7. Percy helped Charlie Rooster get unstuck from Johnny Mouse's "house" hole.

8. They helped each other decide that it was not the best idea to spend the night together; instead, they could dream about each other, as true friends do!

When Friends Help Each Other, They Are Cooperating

Explain the above statement to the class. Ask your students to give examples of how they help each other (cooperate) in the classroom. Add their replies to the butcher paper.

Hand out a "Friendship Wheel" (page 197) to each student.

Give the following directions:

1. In the center, where the smaller circle is located, draw a picture of yourself and label it with your name.

2. Think of four friends that you help, or that help you. Write their names in the four sections.

3. Draw a picture and/or write a sentence expressing how you or your friend help each other.

4. Share the wheels either with the rest of the class or small groups. Display the wheels.

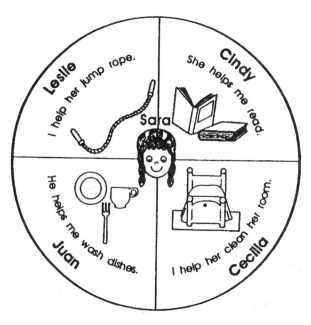

Friendship Wheel

See suggested activity on page 196.

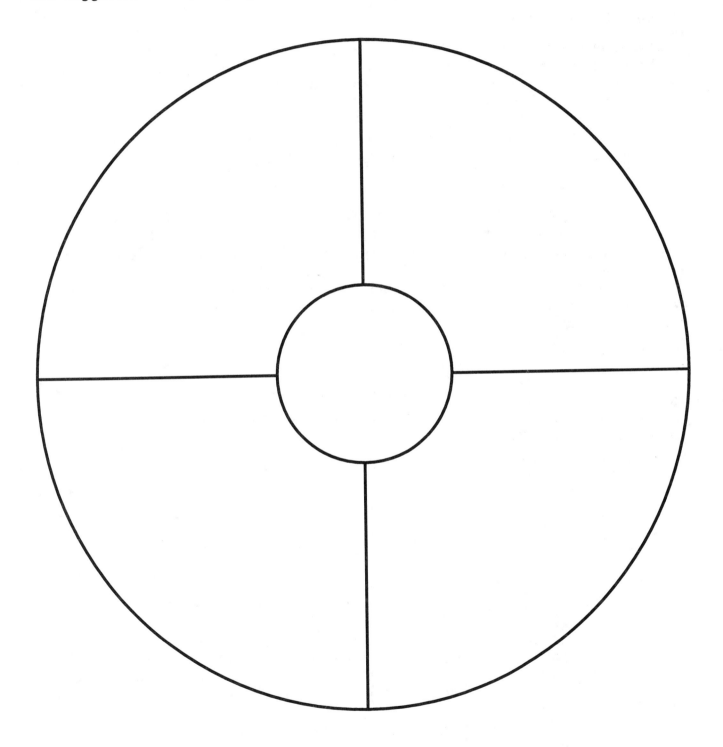

Writing Activities

Note: To help your students reach their maximum writing potential, enlist the help of volunteers or aides during the language experiences.

My Friends Book

After discussing the concept of friendship, a My Friends book will give your students an opportunity to tell about their friends in a written form. Use the writing sheet (page 199) and reproduce five or six per student. Hand out the copies and allow enough time for your students to complete their pages. When finished, give each student two sheets of colored construction paper for front and back covers. Allow them to decorate their covers as desired, being sure to include the title "My Friends." Have the class share their books orally, and then place them in a reading area for all to enjoy!

Friendship Means . . . Accordion Book

To make an accordion book, fold several 12" x 18" (30.48 cm x 45.72 cm) pieces of colored paper in half. Tape the edges together to form accordion pages. Completed books can be folded for easy storage. At the top of each page have the students write "Friendship means . . . ." At the bottom of each page tell the students to complete the sentence. (For example, *Friendship means . . . having someone to play with*, . . . *sharing your favorite toys*, or . . . *spending time with someone you like*.) Let the children illustrate their pages. For younger students, write down the text they dictate and allow them to illustrate the pages.

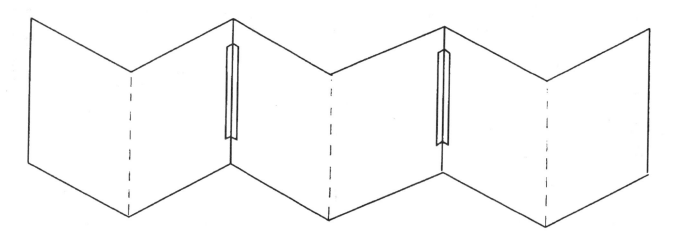

Be a Friend Poster

The definition of a poster, according to Webster's Dictionary, is "a large public advertisement or notice posted publicly." Discuss this meaning with your students. Explain that you are going to "hire" them to create a poster for a school "ad campaign." The campaign slogan is "How to Be a Friend." Provide each student with a large piece of tagboard or butcher paper. Review ways in which friends can help each other by looking at the completed friendship wheels (page 197). Provide markers, crayons, chalk, and/or paints for students to create their posters. Display the posters in "public view" by placing them in the hallways, library, lunchroom, and bathrooms around school.

Note: You can form poster teams of three or four to create a single poster.

My Friend

_____ is my friend.

My friend likes to eat _____

_____

My friend likes to play _____

_____

When we are together, we like to _____

_____

I like to help my friend. I help my friend _____

_____

My friend is_____
years old.

My friend has_____
sisters and
_____brothers.

I like my friend!

A picture of my friend.

Poetry

Friends Are Fun Acrostic

An acrostic poem is a wonderful writing experience that encourages students to expand their vocabularies. As a class, write a sample acrostic on the board. Then, just for fun, allow the students to sit anywhere in the room to write their own acrostics. Tell them to use the names of friends as the bases for their acrostics. Ask for volunteers to share their poems.

Display the poems in the hallway so that other school friends may enjoy them too!

A "Round" of Song

A song is often written in a rhyming form. Teach the simple song below (set to the tune of "Row, Row, Row Your Boat"). After the students become familiar with the lyrics, divide the class into two teams. Teach the song as a round in which a second group begins singing after the first group finishes the first line. If your students seem to enjoy a two-part round, divide teams again and try a four-part friendship sing-a-thon!

> *Love, love, love your friends,*
> *Different as they seem.*
> *Playing, laughing, joking, helping,*
> *True friends are in our dreams!*

Cooperation Chant

This cooperation chant has a strong rhythm. After your students learn the words, they can say the chant while "marching" to the lunchroom, bus, or a special activity.

1. We are friends, yes we are,
   Cooperation is our star!
   To the left and to the right,
   We will help you to be bright!

2. We are friends, yes we are,
   Cooperation is our star!
   To the sky and to the ground,
   We will praise you all around!

3. We are friends, yes we are,
   Cooperation is our star!
   To the east and to the west,
   Cooperating is the BEST!

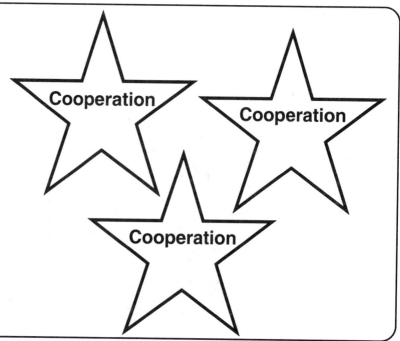

Language Arts—Cooperation Cards

Teacher Directions: Divide the class into teams of four or five. Reproduce enough Cooperation Cards (pages 201 and 202) to give each team two or three. Give the teams five minutes to cooperate and discuss how they would work together to solve the problems on the cards. Let the groups share their solutions with the rest of the class through a discussion period.

Language Arts—Cooperation Cards *(cont.)*

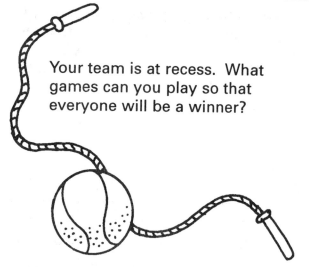

Your team is at recess. What games can you play so that everyone will be a winner?

There is a new student in your class. How can you become friends with him or her?

Your team is going on a picnic in the park. What will each person bring?

Your teacher wants your team to make a dinosaur mural. Who will draw what?

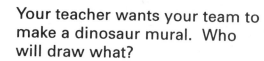

Your team is watching cartoons. How can everyone get to see what they want?

A friend's dad is planting a vegetable garden. How can your team help?

Science—How Are We Different?

Our bodies are growing every day. Friends grow and change at different rates. Find out ways that you are the same or different from your friends.

Hypothesis

Check one:

_____I am different from my friends in many ways.

_____I am the same as my friends.

Procedure

Fill in the chart after using the correct measuring method.

What to Measure . . .	My Name	Friend One	Friend Two	Measuring Method
Measure your arm from your elbow to your fingertips.				
Measure your body from your head to your heels.				
Take your pulse. How many times does it beat in one minute?				
Measure the length of your foot from your heel to your toes.				

Results

Use your chart to fill in the blanks.

My arm is longer than_____. My arm is shorter than_____.

I am taller than_____. I am shorter than_____.

My heart beats faster than_____. My heart beats slower than_____.

My foot is longer than_____. My foot is shorter than_____.

Conclusion

Circle the correct response.

1. My friends and I are different.

2. My friends and I are the same.

Friendly Fractions

Directions: Pretend that you have a bag of cookies that you need to share with your friends. Divide up the cookies for two, three, and four people.

1. Color each ½ brown.   **2. Color each ⅓ yellow.**   **3. Color each ¼ red.**

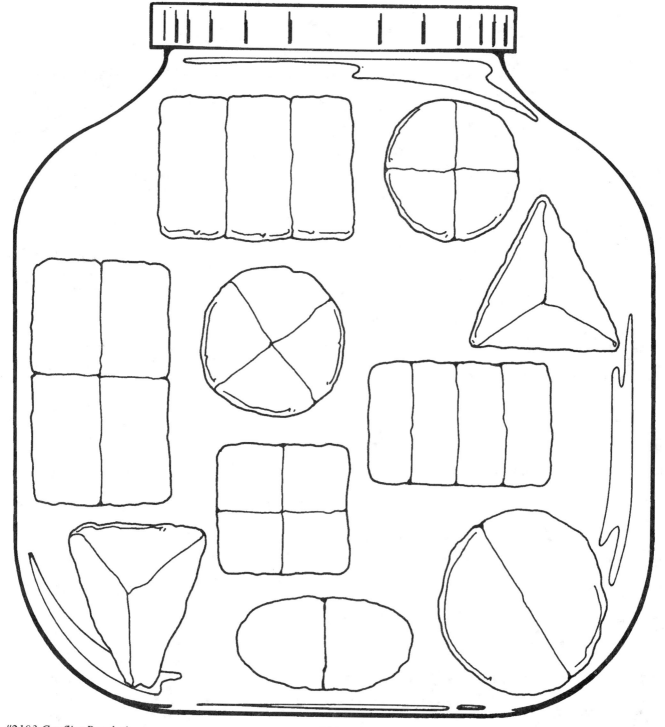

A Cooperative Concert

The definition of an *orchestra* is a group of people playing music together by cooperating.

The orchestra puts on a concert.

Create a cooperation concert by having your students become the musicians. Let them take turns at leading as the concert conductor!

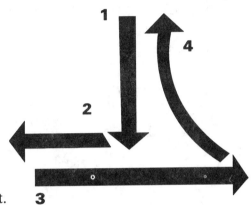

The musicians are responsible for playing their instruments and cooperating with the conductor.

The conductor is responsible for leading the cooperating concert.

To create your orchestra, divide the class into four groups. Each group will play instruments from one of the four sections:

Baton Movement

Percussion	Woodwinds	Brass	Strings
cymbal drum triangle sticks xylophone	flute kazoo recorder whistle	horn trumpet bugle	autoharp guitar ukulele violin

Note: If your students cannot play real instruments, substitute with homemade or toy versions!

Have your students sit in chairs or on the floor according to the diagram below. Explain that they are not to play unless the conductor signals to them. This is how the orchestra cooperates with each other and the conductor.

The conductor has four signals to tell his or her orchestra what to do. They are all done with his or her hands.

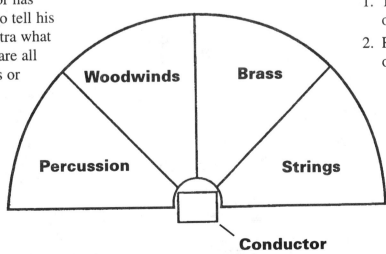

Conductor Signals:

1. Taps desk with baton—orchestra becomes quiet.

2. Raises both arms in the air—orchestra prepares to play.

3. Points with one hand to a particular section—that section begins to play.

4. Keeps everyone on the same beat by completing baton movement (above) with other hand.

Friendship Exercise Course

To complete the Friendship Exercise Course divide the class into friendship teams of two. When the teams have completed the course, have cool treats waiting to celebrate their successes! To set up the course activities, follow the diagram below. Enlist the help of adults to stand as monitors throughout the course area.

START

Activity 1: Three-Legged Run (Teams tie adjacent legs together and run around three cones.)

FINISH LINE

Activity 2: Throw-a-Ball-a-Thon (Teams toss balls into the air 50 times while counting.)

Activity 5: Cycle Fun (Teams ride big wheel tricycles on a circular or linear course.)

Activity 6: Gunnysack Race (Team members get into the same sack and hop as quickly as they can to the finish line!)

Activity 4: Crazy Walk (Teams walk on a balance beam or masking-taped line, backwards!)

Activity 3: Sailboat Race (Teams blow small boats across a wading pool.)

Culminating Friendship Activities

These activities are appropriate culminating activities for the friendship unit.

Friendship Quilt

Divide a white cloth sheet into squares according to the number of students in the class. Cut along the fold lines to give each student his or her own individual square. Using permanent marking pens, have the students draw their faces and names on their squares.

Note: Be sure to warn them to draw their faces and names away from the edges so that when the quilt is sewn together they will not lose any of their drawings! Ask a parent volunteer to sew the squares together. Display the friendship quilt in the classroom or a hallway!

Friendship Sack Lunches

Divide the students into sack lunch teams. Provide a brown lunch bag for each teammate. Have them decorate their bags and write the names of both partners on them. Explain that each teammate will be making a lunch for his or her partner and bringing it to school to share with him or her. Send information letters home with the students along with the bags they have decorated for their partners. Ask the parents to help their children make the lunches (including a sandwich, a fruit, and a dessert). During lunch on the designated day, have the sack lunch teams switch their lunch bags and eat together in the classroom, lunchroom, or outside. (Be aware of dietary restrictions before switching lunches.) Ask a parent volunteer to make some punch as a lunchtime beverage.

Animal Friends

Animals are our friends, too. Ask the students if they would like to bring in their animal friends from home. Make arrangements with the students' parents to bring in pet friends for a show-and-tell time. Have the students tell the class about their special friends, including the ways they take care of, share, cooperate,

Resources and References

CCRC (Children's Creative Response to Conflict)

P.O. Box 271

Nyack, NY 10960

(914) 358-4601

Children's Creative Response to Conflict presents many kinds of teacher training programs throughout the United States. As an extension of their standard workshops and courses, they will custom-design workshops to meet a group's time and theme requirements. Their handbooks, *The Friendly Classroom for a Small Planet* by Priscilla Prutzman et al., is a wonderful resource. In addition to many creative lesson plans and ideas, it lists dozens of regional CCRC branches and related programs. Also available are a newsletter, *Sharing Space*, and a literature service featuring books, articles, and a slide show on the CCRC program.

Sunburst Communications

101 Castleton Street

P.O. Box 40

Pleasantville, NY 10570-9807

Phone: 1-800-431-1934

FAX: (914) 769-2109

Sunburst Communications offers videos, games, newsletters and posters for grades K–12 on various subjects of guidance and health. They offer several videos specifically on conflict resolution. Request a catalog for more details about their products.

❖ Canter, Lee and Katia Petersen. *Teaching Students to Get Along*. Lee Canter and Associates, 1995.

❖ Faber, Adele and Elaine Mazlish. *How to Talk so Kids Can Learn: At Home and in School*. Rawson Associates, 1995.

❖ Gardner, Howard. *Frames of Mind: The Theory of Multiple Intelligences*. Basic Books, 1983.

❖ Porro, Barbara. *Talk It Out: Conflict Resolution in the Elementary Classroom*. Association for Supervision and Curriculum Development, 1996.

❖ Prutzman, Priscilla, et al. *The Friendly Classroom for a Small Planet: A Handbook on Creative Approaches to Living and Problem Solving*. New Society Publishers, 1988.